INTRODUCTION

The "Nuts & Bolts" of Body Piercing is a handbook and resource guide for the beginning body piercer. It connects the dots between how to get started in the body piercing business and learning the essential techniques of "how to" perform a body piercing on a real person.

It is a collection of my hands-on experiences, observations, and conclusions, in the body piercing industry over the past 15 years and personally performing tens of thousands of body piercings.

This is extremely important because I had the benefit of examining the same clients over a period of years to observe the long-term results of their piercings. Since there are no universal standards of how to properly perform a body piercing taught by the body piercing industry, this experience over time is the only standard we have to verify that our techniques of body piercing pass the test of time.

As a new piercer, the exclusive, insider information contained in this book is exactly what you need to know but cannot get from other body piercers.

Most of you already know, "They" do not share valuable body piercing information with inexperienced, or new body piercers. *The "Nuts & Bolts" of Body Piercing* is also a companion to the body piercing demonstration videos found at http://www.how2pierce.com.

The body piercing demonstration videos are designed to show specific technique(s) or body piercing procedure(s). *The "Nuts & Bolts" of Body Piercing* helps to fill in the gaps between the demonstration videos and specific information you must have. The handbook and demonstration videos, together, provide a more complete picture of what every new body piercer needs to know.

Jerry Frederick
Body Piercer

© 2010 Jerry Frederick/Body Creations - ALL RIGHTS RESERVED

TABLE OF CONTENTS

Chapter 1 - Body Piercing Resource Guide 3

Chapter 2 - Welcome to Your Next Obsession 11

Chapter 3 - Body Piercing "Speak" 15

Chapter 4 - The Power of Probing Questions 21

Chapter 5 - Proper Hand Washing Techniques 26

Chapter 6 - Cross-Contamination the 800 lb. Gorilla 28

Chapter 7 - Clean to Contaminated 32

Chapter 8 - Autoclave Is Your Most Important Instrument 35

Chapter 9 - Oops Where is That Needle 38

Chapter 10 – Common Piercing Questions Answered 41

Chapter 11 - Body Piercing Aftercare Suggestions 48

Chapter 12 - Understanding Licensing and Certification 52

Chapter 13 – Jewelry Standards in Body Piercing 57

Chapter 14 - Successful Stretching Discussed 61

Chapter 15 - Specific Details & Tips For Each Piercing 64

Chapter 16 – Body Piercing Migration and Rejection 75

Chapter 17 - Bloodborne Pathogens & CPR Certification 78

Chapter 18 - Dealing with Problems, Emergencies & Needle Sticks 82

Chapter 1 – Body Piercing Resource Guide

The Body Piercing Resource Guide is a very thorough listing of supplies, tools and equipment you will use if you expect to become a body piercing business owner, or an independent contractor working in someone else's shop.

This list provides you with a guide to a well-equipped body piercing shop/studio. As a business owner you will use most, if not all of these items. If you are an independent contractor, this list will help you obtain specific items you will need.

The right column is the estimated costs for each item and the quantity it is purchased in. These prices are estimates of cost at the time this book is written.

Prices can be negotiated. In some cases the prices in the estimated column will be higher on some items, and may be lower on other items, but this will allow you to create your initial estimated costs for these items as you check with suppliers.

You will save a lot of money if you shop for the very best deals and don't be afraid to ask for a better price on items you feel may be a little pricy. For instance, gloves have a big range of prices for the same case of gloves.

I have generated a comprehensive Vendor List for you to use.

This list of vendors was created to aid you in making informed decisions on the purchase of body jewelry, related items and services. I deal with these vendors and have been satisfied with their prices, products, and services. We have reviewed the items we use, however, if you will investigate each company, you will likely find other items that will benefit your business. Therefore, don't limit your self to just the items we purchase.

The author of this list has absolutely no financial interest in any items you may purchase; therefore the method of receiving this referral to any company you contact can be totally anonymous if you choose. Many of the vendors mentioned in this list are small business owners and are extremely helpful and eager to assist with your needs. Don't hesitate to use these valuable resources to help your piercing business grow.

Item	Estimated Price/Quanities
Table Paper	$26.00 /Case
Disposable Lint-Free Wash Cloths	$16.00/ Case
Dispenser for Wash Cloths	$29.99
Medi Q-Tips	$9.99/ 1000 pierces
Gauze 2 X 2	$3.99 / pkg of 200 pierces
Bacitracin pks for Stretching	$13.89/ box of 144 individual packs
Cleansing Towelettes (BZK) Wipes	$3.79/ box of 100 pieces
1.3 QT Sharps Container	$4.19 each
Dial Soap for Hand Washing	$20.49 / gallon
SaniCloth HBV Wipes (hard surface cleanser)	$9.99/ Container of 160 wipes
Isopropyl Alcohol	$0.99/ 16 oz
Foam Hard Surface Cleaner	$5.99/ 18 oz.
Madacide Disinfectant	27.49/ gal.
Instant Cold Packs	$47.99/ 100 bewell@bewell.com (for unusual swelling after piercing)
3-1/2 X 9 Jewelry Pouches	$9.79/ box of 200
2-1/4 X 4 Needle & Jewelry Pouch	$8.50/ box of 200
5-1/4 X 10 Jewelry & Tool Pouch	$20.00/ box of 200
Pliers	$5.00 each
Needles	$0.25 average each one all sizes
Infectious Waste Bags (Biohazard)	$19.99/ box of 100
Techni-Care Surgical Scrub (or similar type)	$19.99/ doz. Of 16 oz bottles
Facial Tissues	$25.00/ Case (Buy at Costco/Sams Club)
Latex Gloves	$45 / Case - 10 boxes/case - 100 gloves /box
18 gallon Step-Open Trash Can	$105.89 each (may find at Home Depot, but Medical grade is better)
Stainless Steel Hemostat Holder	$38.79 ea. (Holds marketing pen, calipers, hemostats, etc.)
Calipers	$24.98 each
Biohazard Instrument tray w/ cover	$31.79 ea. (Holds/secures used piercing tools before soakin)
Mayo Stand	$49.00 on ebay
Sundry jars for Piercing Table	$39.49/ 5 piece set
Stainless Steel Ointment Jars	$13.99 ea. (holds bacitracin pks, rubber bands, misc.items)
Ritter M7 Speed Clav	Check Autoclave Chapter on how to buy an Autoclave
UltraSonic 9-3/8 X 5-3/8 X 4	$329.99 Size is more important than price (mush hold your tools)
Forceps, Ring Opening/Closing Pliers	$5.00 each
Hemostats, Nostril/Needle Receiving Tubes	$2.50 each
Wire Wheel Gauge	$18.50 each
Steel Piecing Cart w/ Wheels	$491.39 - look for 5-drawer tool chest from Sears (or similar store). Drawers should be at least a MINIMUM of 3 inches deep - Cart must be steel so it can be sterilized using hard surface disinfectants
#10 Rubber Bands 1-1/4 X 1/16	$4.95 /lb.- approximately 3700 pierces per pound (Internet Search)
Toothpicks (round)	$0.99/ box
Paper C-Fold Towels	$25.00/ case - approximately 2500 towels per case (Sam's Club)
Ultrasonic Cleaning Tablets	$34.95/ 64 tablets
Toilet Paper	$15.00/ case (54 rolls per case)
Corks (Medical Rubber)	$2.20/ 100 pierces in bag - $20 minimum order (get 1/2 inch corks)
Disposable Dental Bibs (Plastic Back)	$20/ case (provide plastic barrier between your piercing set up and mayo stand. Use one as a mayo stand barrier for inserting or removing jewelry - Then dispose of after use.
Medicine Plastic Cups (1 oz)	$19.50/ case - Dose Cups approximately 1000 per case
Antibacterial Hand Lotion	$11.99/ 16 oz bottle
Floor Disinfectant/Cleaner	$16.99/ gallon
Gentian Violet (marking Tongue/Genitals)	$5.50/ 2 oz bottle
Pennington/Sponge Clamps	$5.00 each

DISCLAIMER: No implied or express warranty is made to the exact specifications, quality, durability, materials, or certification of the jewelry offered by the companies mentioned for body piercing jewelry. We encourage you to do your own due diligence before purchasing any products from vendors mentioned in this list.

A LIST OF RESOURCES FOR BODY PIERCING JEWELRY, PIERCING SUPPLIES AND MISCELLANEOUS SERVICES FOR YOUR BODY PIERCING BUSINESS

Body Piercing Demonstration Videos - http://www.how2pierce.com

Rubber Bands - Alliance Rubber Company - http://www.alliance-rubber.com
501-262-2700
Select Size #10 rubber bands. Using the #10 size allows for 4 easy wraps around clamps without breaking.

Corks - CAM Supply, Inc - 888-238-0808 - 490 E. Menlo Ave, Hemet, CA 92543 - These are medical rubber corks - They do not split, dry out and safer than a natural cork. In addition they have smooth surfaces and you have no throw-a-ways because of the consistent quality. They have different sizes and large is a good size of all piercings. Large is 1/2 in diameter.

Needles, Receiving Tubes, Tapers, Forceps, Hemostats, Openers, Closers, Pliers, Nostril Bending Pliers, Septum Clamps, Wire Gauge Wheel, Disinfectants, Tool Care, and some basic medical supplies related to body piercing and tattooing.

Industrial Strength (Sharpass Needles) - 877-667-4277 - http://www.isneedles.com - The design of their needles allows for a very smooth exit, producing a more comfortable piercing than with other needles that were designed for drawing fluid from the body, not piercing. I assure you your clients will notice the difference. Excellent service and selection of products.

Autoclave Testing (Steam Sterilizer Testing Kit) - North Bay Bioscience LLC - 800-289-7786 - http://www.nbbs.com - They send your results very month instead of every test like others do. This is much easier on paperwork and keeping you compliant. they will also send your results to your professional organization (APP) if you are a member. APP requires autoclave test be sent to them as a condition of membership, so this is very handy.

Medical Supplies - Henry Schein - 135 Duryea Road - Melville, NY 11747 - 800-851-0400 - 800-972-2611 order dept.
Call them and open an account. They will give you the name and number of your sales rep. that you will work with. Request a catalog. As you develop a relationship with your sales rep, you can often get discounts off the catalog price. They have warehouses across the US and your order will usually arrive in one or two days. You may also check with medical supply houses in your local city for your basic needs, like gloves, sterilization pouches, etc. We have listed the measurements of the sterilization pouches you will need to fit your tools. The actual inside dimension is the most important. Sometimes the outside dimension is the same as another pouch, but the inside diminution is too small to hold your tools. So choose your pouches with care because the tools must be placed in your pouch open and unlocked when autoclaving.

Body Jewelry & Piercing Supplies- Metal Mafia - 800-MY MAFIA - http://www.metalmafia.com - Uses 316L Surgical, implant grade steel ASTM-F-138. - Excellent selection of stainless steel internally threaded piercing jewelry. Have a reasonable selection of titanium (barbells, rings, & labrets. Great Prices! Wide selection of dermal anchor threaded ends and tools for inserting dermal anchors. Can buy anchors in bulk, that really reduces the price per anchor. Excellent Service! Big supply of ear stretching jewelry

Body Jewelry - NeoMetal - 2916 NW Buckin Hill Rd. #283 - Silverdale, WA 98383 - 800-471-7791
Titanium jewelry - small "mini" labrets are threadless. Use this jewelry for facial, ear, beauty mark, and lip piercings. It is a little pricy, but we have found clients will pay for it. Excellent selection of colored stones for gem ends.

Body Jewelry - The Object Maker - 877-666-9166 - http://www.theobjectmaker.com - 14 and 18K nostril screws with CZ and Diamond stones. Excellent pricing and workmanship. Brian - owner and craftsman and super guy to work with.

Body Jewelry - Industrial Strength Body Jewelry - (not the same Industrial Strength for needles) - 800-339-5725 - they are pricy but very high quality jewelry. You will find practically any body piercing product you will ever need. Have great anodized titanium jewelry. Huge catalog.

Body Jewelry - Body Gems - 877-263-9436 - http://www.bodygems.com - 14k Yellow or White Gold Jewelry - Nickel Free
Huge Selection - Reasonable prices for gold. Excellent service.

Body Jewelry - Body Vision Los Angeles - http://www.bodyvision.net - 909-596-1802 - Excellent source for gold jewelry. Unique designs, moderately priced - high quality workmanship - made to order so it takes a little time to get delivery, but desire to satisfy is excellent.

Body Jewelry - Streamline Jewelry - http://www.streamlinejewelry.com - 800-548-1282 - Reasonably priced with a wide selection of body jewelry. Best for your retail body jewelry. Limited selection in stainless steel internally threaded piercing jewelry. Selection of dermal anchor tools. They are just a big company but have a large selection of body jewelry that others do not have.

Autoclave (Refurbished) - http://www.sterilizers.com/refurbished.asp - Perform an internet search for used autoclave and check out Ebay or Craig's List in your area.

Body Piercing Organization - Association of Professional Piercers - http://www.safepiercing.org - A wide variety of body piercing information is available from this organization.

Body Jewelry & Piercing Supplies - Le Roi - 888-298-7766 - http://www.LeRoi.com - They have a great stainless steel taper kit for jewelry insertion. You can insert pin or dimple jewelry using the same taper in each gauge. This is the only place to get JUMBO SIZE JEWELRY (bigger than 00 gauge) that I am aware of.

H2Ocean Aftercare Products - Justin - 877-858-1234 - Tucson, Arizona - Justin provides excellent service.

Aftercare Products - Care-Tech Laboratories - 800-325-9681 - www.caretechlabs.com - You can purchase Tech 2000 mouthwash for Tongue piercing aftercare and Satin Antimicrobial Soap for piercing aftercare in conjunction with sea salt soaks.

Professional Insurance - PPIB (Professional Program Insurance Brokerage) 415-898-4242 - They provide piercing and tattoo liability insurance and business insurance.

Body jewelry is measured in fractions of 1/16th of an inch. Here is a quick reference chart of jewelry measurements in order from the smallest to the largest..

Jewelry Measurements		Fractions in 16th
1/8	=	2/16
3/16	=	3/16
1/4	=	4/16
5/16	=	5/16
3/8	=	6/16
7/16	=	7/16
1/2	=	8/16
9/16	=	9/16
5/8	=	10/16
11/16	=	11/16
3/4	=	12/16
13/16	=	13/16
7/8	=	14/16
15/16	=	15/16
1 inch	=	16/16

The following is a chart converting US measurements to the metric system. Many manufactures use the metric system so this will help you convert to US measurements to metric.

Gauge	TO	Millimeter
18 g.		1.0 mm

Gauge	mm
16 g.	1.2 mm
14 g.	1.6 mm
12 g.	2.1 mm
10 g.	2.6 mm
8 g.	3.2 mm
6 g.	4.2 mm
4 g.	5.2 mm
2 g.	6.5 mm
0 g.	8.0 mm
00 g.	9.5 mm
000 g.	10. mm

The following is a chart converting the American System of Measurements to Metric. This is very helpful when ordering ear stretching jewelry or Captive Bead Rings.

Internal Diameter	External Millimeters
1/8	3.0 mm
5/32	3,9 mm
3/16	4.8 mm
1/4	6.0 mm
5/16	8.0 mm
3/8	9.5 mm
7/16	11 mm
Slightly Less> 1/2	12 mm
1/2	13 mm
9/16	14 mm
5/8	16 mm

This is Where Teflon Tape helps to bridge the gap between 5/8 and 3/4 plugs, and so on with bigger sizes.

3/4	19 mm
7/8	22 mm
1 inch	25 mm

Dealing With Suppliers and Vendors

Most suppliers and vendors will require some type of prepayment (credit card, money order or certified check) when they first start dealing with you. Don't be offended, it happens to everybody. You may want to start with small orders at first to demonstrate you are good customer. After you have developed a good report with the merchant, they will likely send you product and let you pay COD.

I like COD because I know my inventory is always paid for and I don't have a debt to pay later . . . the COD fee is a pain but better than building up a large credit card balance.

Buy basic piercing jewelry first, then start branching out into other types of piercing jewelry as you can afford it. Make sure that you have proper piercing supplies, so you don't risk cross-contamination by trying to make-do with non-sterile supplies.

© 2010 Jerry Frederick/Body Creations - ALL RIGHTS RESERVED

Chapter 2 - Welcome To Your Next Obsession

There is something about adorning oneself that can become addictive - from jewelry to shoes and even tattoos. It has to do with adding that little extra touch that gives you individuality shows personality or frankly, just looks great! On a physiological level the addictive nature all stems from the same thing. When you shop, or get a piercing or tattoo, natural endorphins or feel good chemicals are released into your body, and because it makes us happy—we keep going back for more.

Welcome To Your Next Obsession has been our company motto for the past 15 years. That is why _training_ is so important to give your clients the best experience you can give. If you do they will come back on a regular basis and bring their friends. That's when you will have a successful body piercing practice.

Develop a Strong Relationship Between Piercer & Piercee

A strong relationship . . . makes a more positive piercing experience. Everything evolves from the relationship between the body piercer and the piercee. The piercee's "warm and fuzzy" experience depends upon the piercers ability make the piercee feel comfortable.

The piercer must create an atmosphere of professionalism. If the piercee acknowledges that professionalism, then, a relationship begins and both people have a good chance of developing a long-term business relationship.

As a body piercer, we must develop a feeling of comfort and confidence with the piercee. In many cases this must be done in 30 seconds or less . . . the time it takes a potential piercee to mentally process your attitude, appearance, and professionalism. That evaluation happens instantly and must be positive before the piercee consciously approves of doing business with you, ultimately trusting you enough to allow you to stick a needle in them.

Success for a body piercer is determined by the lasting relationships between the piercer and the piercee. To operate a successful body piercing business you must retain between 60 to 80 percent repeat and referral business. That means developing positive relationships with your clients is a must to maintain a long term body piercing business.

Body Piercing is More Than Just Poking Holes

Body piercing is "creating a home" in a person's body for an inanimate piece of body jewelry. Body jewelry must be placed in the body so that it rests comfortably in the body with no resistance from the body . . . this is why knowing how to pierce, proper placement, quality of jewelry, and correct jewelry gauge, diameter and length is critical to a successful piercing.

When you think about body piercing in this way . . . it makes a lot more sense why just any pierce of body jewelry is not good enough. This is just another reason why good body piercers will not let you bring body jewelry in "off the street" for you to be pierced with. Jewelry selection and placement determine the initial success of the piercing.

The Specific Knowledge You Need to be a Body Piercer

As with any profession you need to master certain information unique to body piercing. That information includes but not limited to:

- Sterilization from beginning to end
- How to deal with people, gain their trust and put them at ease
- Then you can discuss with your client when a particular piercing is not a good choice for that individual
- You need to know the healing times and appropriate aftercare for each piercing
- Consequently, you need to know which piercing tools and techniques for each piercing
- How to prepare and mark all of the piercings you are qualified to perform
- The best jewelry designs and proper materials for each
- The names and locations of traditional piercings.

Earn a Reputation As A Safe Piercer by Following These Guidelines

Safety is the single most important requirement of any piercer. That means never put your client or yourself at risk in any way. Your reputation as a safe piercer will be an extremely valuable asset. Follow these guidelines:

- Sterilization and hygiene must be strictly observed
- Never do a piercing that might endanger the pierce or insert a pierce of jewelry that is inappropriate regardless of what the client might desire.
- Never use an ear-piercing GUN to pierce anything. Period!

- Never do a piercing under the influence of drugs or alcohol.
- Never pierce anyone who is intoxicated.

Sadly No University or Training Facilities for Body Piercing

Sadly there are no Universities, State Colleges, Communities Colleges, or Technical Schools where you can learn the skills and techniques of body piercing. Surprisingly, there are no industry-sponsored programs to help you learn the art of body piercing either.

That leaves it up to YOU, to try and find help, in your quest to learn more about how to pierce.

It is obvious, at this time, if you are going to learn how to pierce, you must learn it from watching someone else who knows how. If you can learn it face-to-face with a mentor that is great and desirable. However, if you do not have a personal mentor, you need to find other means to learn how to pierce. Most people tell me that they end up feeling overwhelmed, frustrated and ready to give up.

Help is on the way. As you read this book, you will discover all the tips and tricks about body piercing that we have learned over the past 15 years. This is inside information that you would only get if your were working in someone's perching shop by listening and observing everything that is going on.

In addition, we reveal our prized piercing resources, giving you a list of our vendors, medical suppliers, and other valuable contacts. A lot of time is spent helping you find reasonable prices on the items you need to buy for your body piercing endeavors saving you a lot of money.

This book is written to compliment the piercing demonstrations videos found at http://www.how2pierce.com. In this publication you will find information you will never get by just watching and observing piercings. The Book on *The "Nuts & Bolts" of Body Piercing* is full of information that would take you years to accumulate by actively working in the body piercing business. Most importantly, this information conveys an insider's knowledge, giving you a unique understanding of what the body piercing business is all about.

If you want to move forward in the body perching business, the information is right in front of you. Read it, every word is important to your body piercing activities, and vital in generating a long career in body piercing.

© 2010 Jerry Frederick/Body Creations - ALL RIGHTS RESERVED

Chapter 3 – Body Piercing "Speak"

What to Say and What Not to Say For a Successful Body Piercing Career!

In all of my Body Piercing Demonstration Materials, and conversations working with clients during piercings you will observe that I use very general language. There is a reason for that. General terms are used so no one can "Fence You In" or "Corner You" into an indefensible or uncomfortable position.

There are very few "absolutes" in the body piercing business. That is why I use the word "generally" often.

For instance, people can heal their piercing many different ways, and somebody out there has used some product to heal their piercing successfully that you strongly suggest that they not use. In some cases people don't use anything to heal a piercing and do it successfully. If you make an absolute statement, "you cannot heal your piercing with that particular substance, someone out there can prove you wrong.

During your piercing career you will learn to pierce a certain way. It is a way you feel comfortable with and is successful for you. That does not mean other ways will not work too. An example would be, you don't feel a certain piercing should be done free hand, but somebody else always does that piercing free hand and seems to be successful with the piercing. Again this is an issue you can fuss and fight over all day long and you both would probably be right.

I am not a big fan of free-hand piercings and OSHA is certainly not a fan of free-hand piercings but for now let's get back to protecting your backside with careful, general-in-nature conversations with your clients.

Avoid arguments at all costs. As the piercer you will never win an argument . . . at least winning arguments will not pay your bills. Avoiding arguments means never talk in "Statements" or "Absolutes" with your clients and other piercers. Learn to temper your statements with questions. Questions take the edge and argument out of the important point you are trying to make. We will cover Questions versus Statements later in this chapter.

Don't misunderstand, you must communicate proper aftercare, jewelry selection, and a host of other information to you client, and you expect your client to follow your suggestions. The key is how you communicate that information to them that makes you a hero instead of a zero.

Your words will make or break your body piercing business. Proper, persuasive and totally accurate communication with your clients should be given a great deal of thought and preparation. Your entire body-piercing career will revolve around explaining the concept of body piercing to your clients. This means how to successfully wear and enjoy their body jewelry.

Wearing body jewelry is *much* different than wearing a ring on your finger or wearing a bracelet or necklace.

Body jewelry is a foreign object placed into the body. The body must adjust and co-exist with the body jewelry. The body does not have any responsibility when you slip a finger ring, bracelet or necklace on. The body acts only as a structure that is adorned with jewelry hanging from it. The body does not react to this type of jewelry, unless, for instance a ring is too tight on your finger. You simply remove the tight ring and the problem is solved.

When body jewelry does not fit correctly, the body starts reacting and communicating with you immediately. It communicates by becoming red, swollen, and festered - producing liquid discharge. If the problem is not corrected the jewelry can migrate out of the body leaving a scar behind.

When selecting appropriate jewelry for a body piercing, always select gauge, diameter, or length that will easily co-exist in the placement of the body jewelry.

In addition, high-traffic areas of the body such as navels need special consideration when selecting jewelry. High-traffic areas get a lot of movement from the jewelry and thicker jewelry is necessary to reduce irritation. Play areas such as nipples and genitals also require thicker jewelry to avoid severe discomfort from play.

Discuss with your client the concept of how their body must adjust to and co-exist with the jewelry you insert into their piercing. If they understand that the body is conforming to the jewelry, they will understand that the jewelry you select is very important, and *must* be of a certain size and gauge.

Therefore, don't let other piercers intimidate you, just because they put big, unattractive jewelry in their clients. Don't let that persuade you to do the same. They are not doing their clients a good job by putting big gaudy jewelry in their piercings.

Words Have Meaning - Your Income Depends Upon Them

The best body piercing success tip I can give you is to learn "how to talk" at the front counter and in the piercing room. In body piercing, words have important meanings and those meanings can make your business or break your business.

In the body piercing business **what** you say and **how** you say it is just as important as the particular piercing skills you possess.

The words you use project security, safety, confidence, experience and skill to every one of your clients. Your selection of words will either create fear in your clients or comfort them making the piercing experience a happy one.

Your piercing client is frightened and apprehensive from the moment they walk into your door, if not then, at least by the time they make the walk back into your piercing room.

Never Use These Words with Your Clients

Everything you say and do must be comforting to the piercing client. That means there are certain works you *never* use. This takes some training and discipline on your part but you will thank yourself if you delete these words from your body-piercing lexicon.

Those words are:

HURT

PAIN

OOPS

BLEEDING

RECOMMEND

When people walk into a piercing studio, they are very susceptible to suggestion, both from you and those accompanying them. Consequently, the words you use are very important.

Your piercing client will ask: Does it hurt? Your answer is: You will feel pressure, that's about all. If they persist: You just say: "It is a pressure piercing, that's about all you will feel. It's just like pinching yourself quickly and letting go".

If you do the piercing right, that is all they will feel. Basically, all they are experiencing is the feel of the "drag of the needle" going through their tissue. This is where the feeling of "pressure" comes from. Train yourself to avoid these words at all costs.

How to Talk with Your Body Piercing Clients

Train yourself to avoid using the word PAIN with your body piercing clients. Substitute the word DISCOMFORT instead of using the word pain.

Your conversation could go something like this. *Sure you could experience some discomfort. Most people experience pressure. That's about all the sensation you will have.*

Or you could say, if you experience any discomfort at all, it will be just a little pressure. Although it is difficult to eliminate the word FEEL from your vocabulary, I try to substitute the word EXPERIENCE for FEEL as often as I can. Experience something is a lot more exciting than feel something. Experiencing "a thing" has a fun connotation, while "a feeling" has a dual meaning. Could be good, but generally means bad feelings.

It is never a good idea to use the word OOPS during a piercing. That tells your client something is wrong. Not a good thing in the piercing room. Train yourself not to react to what is going on with the piercing. Your conversation during the piercing, if any, should be comforting and reassuring to your client.

Asking How Do You Feel . . . Not a Particularly Good Idea

Consider not asking your client "How are you doing" or "How do you feel". If you ask those questions, you are asking clients to evaluate themselves and give you a thoughtful response. You don't want that. You want your client to be thinking, "that wasn't so bad.

When asking "diagnostic" questions of your client, be prepared for an answer you might not like. Make positive statements; don't ask questions about your client's feelings. If you do have to ask a question, just look at them, smile and ask, OK? That is a benign question that does not require an answer. Asking OK means you might get a Yes or No answer, short and sweet. If you ask, "How are you feeling?" You can easily get a dissertation from the client . . . not what you want in the piercing room. Your objective is to visually observe and sense any signs of distress in your client.

Train yourself to make positive statement to your piercing clients, instead of asking probing questions that means a question that requires an answer)! This is totally different than our discussion earlier about not making statements that could incite arguments about jewelry selection or piercing specifics. Making positive statements is completely appropriate and desirable when in the piercing room or tending to your pierced or about to be pierced client.

Try not to use the word BLEEDING in the piercing room. If your client asks if they are bleeding, and they are, just say: "You are oozing just a little. It's going to stop". One problem you will have is a friend or relative in the piercing room blurting out, "You are bleeding." In that case you say: He (or She) is doing just fine. Minimize to the best of your ability what others say in your piercing room. Always offer comforting statements to your piercing client. If you do you will be surprised how many times they tell you, "That didn't hurt at all."

On the other hand, do not "over" comfort your piercing client. If you do, they will stay and stay, and you will never get rid of them. The more you enable them to act hurt, the more they will do it. Don't be an enabler, be a strong positive comforter, and encourage your client to get up and on their way. Understanding your body piercing client and how they react in the piercing room is very important.

Doctors Recommend . . . Piercers Suggest

Want to get into trouble, recommend something, anything, in the piercing business. Do not recommend anything. When piercing, take that word out of your vocabulary forever.

You always SUGGEST! When talking about jewelry or anything about body piercing you only make suggestions. You suggest jewelry size . . . you suggest aftercare procedures . . . you suggest problem assessment solutions . . . you suggest products for aftercare.

You can get into trouble by recommending aftercare products. This can be a liability issue. If you suggest it is unlikely you could be held liable. If you recommend - you are inviting legal liability.

If you offer aftercare products for sale, always suggest their use and have that in your literature. My suggestion is not to Give-Away any aftercare products as an inducement to the piercing. That would suggest that are recommending the aftercare products.

In body piercing there are no generally accepted "published" rules for aftercare or piercing. Therefore, you have no defense by saying you do things the generally accepted method, so use caution when discussing aftercare and piercing with your clients.

© 2010 Jerry Frederick/Body Creations - ALL RIGHTS RESERVED

Chapter 4 - The Power of Probing Questions

Statements Can be Attacked. Questions Can Not be Successfully Attacked.

It is just that simple. As body piercers, when we make statements there is always someone who wants to challenge your statement, and that puts you on the defensive. When you are on the defensive you are not in a strong, positive position to influence the person to do the piercing or have them take you suggestions about a problem piercing.

Questions are open-ended; therefore they are difficult to be attacked. Asking questions puts you on the offensive and in control. Questions make the other person respond.

A question can be asked in such a way that it does not need an answer, but gets the point across. For instance, you suspect a person is using too much sea salt and drying out the tissue around their piercing. Instead of making a statement, "You are using too much sea salt." You could ask a question like this. Could it be that you are using too much sea salt and drying out your skin? That kind of question is totally non-confrontational, and with agreement from the person gives you the answer you are looking for.

There are questions and there are questions

Here is what I mean. It is better to ask questions than make statements. A disarming technique is to ask an indirect question as opposed to asking a direct question. For instance, you see an irritated navel and suspect the person is sleeping on the piercing and severely irritating it. Instead of asking the question, "Are you sleeping on your stomach?" Ask the question. "Is it possible you could be sleeping on your stomach at night and maybe not realizing it?"

You have asked the same question, but the latter question puts you on the side of the piercee. It makes the piercee feel better that you are on their side, yet you are still in control and has said nothing that they can attack. The first, direct question can sound accusatory and make your client feel threatened and uncomfortable.

Using these tactics will help you build your body piercing business successfully. These concepts will also help your body piercing training for counter people and your body piercers.

Vital Questions in Assessing Your Clients Piercing Problems

Here Are Revealing Questions to Ask Your Client When Confronted With Their Piercing Problems. When you ask a question - immediately shut-up and listen carefully to the answer.

If you will ask at least 3 probing questions of your client, they will generally tell you exactly what they are doing to create the problem with their piercing. However, if you do not listen carefully, you will miss what they are saying. Many people simply do not listen carefully after asking a question. They are so eager to rebut what the other person is saying; they totally ignore what their client is actually saying. This is where miscommunication occurs creating frustration in you and your client.

You may find some questions very simple, some redundant, and some way out there. We ask questions many different ways to get the right answers. Think of yourself as Sherlock Holmes. as you attempt to detect problems with a person's piercing. if you are doing the talking, you are losing the battle. Here are the questions:

How old is the piercing?

When did it start acting up?

What was it doing when you first noticed the change in the piercing?

Who did the piercing, i.e. your shop or someone else?

How are you taking care of it (what type of aftercare are they using, if any)

What have you been putting on the piercing to help it heal?

Have you put another persons jewelry in your piercing?

Did you change your jewelry?

How did you sterilize the jewelry before you put it in?

Do you have your original jewelry you were pierced with in the piercing?

Has the piercing been ripped or torn? (eye brow piercings generally migrate out if the piercing is torn or ripped even if just slightly)

Do you sleep on the piercing?

Is the piercing redder in the morning than in the evening? (if so that means they are probably sleeping on it)

Do you belt over the piercing (navel)? (tool belts, gun belts [police, public safety & detention officers], etc)

Do you sit on your job most of the day?

Do you rub your stomach on a display counter at your work?

Do you lift boxes at work? (Women rest boxes they lift on their stomachs irritating navel piercings) (Lifting and carrying children can also irritate a navel piercing)

How often do you clean it each day? (Cleaning too much can be as harmful as not cleaning it enough)

This is so important to your piercing career, lets recap to make sure you are clear on the techniques of asking probing questions.

Asking probing questions will help you discover how you can help your clients. Ask the questions in a non-judgmental manner. Don't act superior . . . your client will quit responding to your efforts to help them.

A Very Simple Technique That Works Every Time

Now you know to always listen, without interruption after, you ask a question. Here's the technique that works every time. Do not verbally respond immediately after your client has responded. This will make them feel like they should keep talking --- this is when you often get the "real" answer.

In other words, an awkward silence makes your client feel they should keep talking and you very often get an honest admission. Just look at them nodding your head in an approving manner and say, what else, Is That All, OK Anything More, That's Interesting What Else Is Happening? You get the idea. Just look at your client, ask a leading question, and then just sit back and listen without interruption.

If you do things to encourage them to keep talking, they will talk themselves out of their accusing tone. Human nature is for them to walk into your studio and insinuate you caused their problem. If you do things to encourage them to keep talking, they will talk themselves out of their accusing tone. The more THEY TALK the easier it is for you to solve their problem.

Persuasion Through Questions Is a Powerful Technique

Making "matter-of-fact statements" to your clients when you are trying to influence them into taking a particular action is strongly discouraged. We never want to put our piercing client on the defensive by making statements that create an uncomfortable reaction from your client. We want to provide our clients with a great service and receive a fair compensation in return. In order to do this you must be able to obtain certain information, or agreement from your client. The way to do that is to ask questions that are to the point and non-threatening. Some suggestions are as follows.

Generally we do this . . . Is that OK with you Generally we find this . . . does that apply to you

A lot of people do this . . . do you like that Many of our clients find this . . . is that all right with you

This jewelry would fit better if . . . wouldn't you agree

Your piercing might heal quicker if . . . don't you agree

It might be better to place the piercing here, don't you think

If you did . . . you might get better results

If we use this jewelry, it would look better, wouldn't you agree?

Can you see how this would fit better?

Doesn't it make sense to . . .

Wouldn't you like it better if . . .

Don't you feel better about . . .

Don't you think your jewelry would look better if . . .

There are many more questions/phrases you can use to avoid being "Fenced In" to a statement you cannot get out of. Try using these terms; I think you will find your body piercing life will be much easier.

© 2010 Jerry Frederick/Body Creations - ALL RIGHTS RESERVED

Chapter 5 - Sanitation Starts With Proper Hand Washing Techniques

Hand washing is considered one of the most effective infection control measures, and easily implemented into your piercing environment. The goal of hand washing is to remove transient microorganisms that might be transmitted to clients, visitors, or piercers or other body modification artists.

You might think hand washing is entirely too simple and unimportant for you to give your attention to, but touching people and things with contaminated hands is the primary way to cross-contaminate your piercing clients and piercing areas.

Any client may harbor microorganisms that are currently harmless to that client, yet could be harmful to another person or to the same client if they find a portal of entry. To prevent the spread of these microorganisms, it is important that hands be washed at the times cited in the lists below.

For Clients Wash Your Hands: Before eating, after using the toilet, after the hands have come in contact with any body substance, such as sputum or drainage from a wound (including a piercing or other body modification), or any mucus membrane.

For Piercers and Other Body Modification Artists Wash Your Hands: Before performing invasive procedures, whether or not gloves are used, before and after contact with wounds, including all forms of modifications, before contact with any body substance or mucus membrane, and between contact with all clients.

During client care, the Center for Disease Control recommends a vigorous hand washing using granule soap, soap-filled tissues or non-microbial liquid soap under a stream of water for at least one minute. The CDC recommends antiseptic hand washing agents when there are known multiple resistant bacteria or before invasive procedures.

Standardized hand washing procedures should be established within the piercing studio because proper hand washing will destroy transit microorganisms on the piercer"s hands and will inhibit cell bacterial growth through the piercing procedure.

Use an Anti-Microbial Soap for Cleaning

Between piercing and piercing related procedures use an ant-microbial soap to reduce excess drying. You will find your hands becoming dry with the continual cleaning, so use an anti-microbial lotion to soften your hands.

Proper Hand Washing Technique

- Take off watch & jewelry
- Adjust the water to a comfortable temperature and flow to prevent spraying
- Wet hands and forearms
- Lather the hands and forearms to 3-4 inches above where the cuff on a glove will reach using a germicidal surgical scrub
- Clean nails and fingers using a scrub brush and germicidal scrub
- Scrub palm and back of same hand to wrist using a circular motion
- All surfaces exposed to the friction of the scrubbing and germicidal
- Continue to wrist, scrubbing in a circular motion
- Repeat for the other hand
- Rinse hands and forearms starting at the fingertips and working toward the elbows keeping hands up and elbows down
- Dry hands with single use, disposable towels
- Glove immediately
-

Completion of prolonged contact with the client should be followed by hand washing performed in the above mentioned manner with the exception of holding the hands downward to allow any microorganisms to flow down the drain.

Chapter 6 - Cross-Contamination The 800 lb. Gorilla In Your Piercing Room

Cross-Contamination is so important it needs a chapter of its own. Understanding and eliminating cross-contamination is the most important issue you will deal with in Body Piercing.

The scope of this book is to make you aware of cross-contamination, and that it should be prevented at all costs in the piercing room and your clean room/area. Since you cannot be observed directly by a knowledgeable piercer, you should make every effort to know your blood-borne pathogens education.

Cross-contamination is the spreading of germs, bacteria and/or disease by carrying them from an infected area to a non-infected area. Cross-contamination prevention is conscientiously acting as to eliminate any chance of spreading bacteria or disease using Universal Precautions.

In body piercing there are no universal rules that everybody is taught and practice, so you will hear multiple opinions from every direction. Everybody has their way of doing things, and they are totally convinced their way is the best and only way. When it comes to cross-contamination there is no middle ground. You either cross-contaminate or you don't. Once you cross-contaminate something your can't take it back. You can correct the error, but once something is contaminated you must immediately take action to eliminate the contamination.

An example of cross-contamination would be if a piercer is wearing protective gloves and then comes in contact with a client's blood, the piercer is generally protected. However, if he answers the phone with those same gloves, the phone has been cross-contaminated with blood-borne pathogens.

If he puts on a new pair of gloves, but then picks something up off the floor and then touches the client, the client has been cross-contaminated with numerous unknown bacteria.

Many uninformed people think they can pick up a needle and start piercing their friends, but there is one key element they do not consider and that is the prevention of cross-contamination. Importantly this is the part that can make you "clients" sick or even kill them, so you need to pay attention to cross-contamination.

Developing sterility awareness means training yourself to see how contamination takes place and take whatever steps are necessary to prevent it. It means taking great pains to always remain constantly alert to what is and is not clean in your environment and thus avoid transferring pathogens from what is not clean to what is clean.

Some people think that transferring human blood is the only way to contaminate your piercing area. Not all-harmful matter is alive. Dead bacteria or particles of dust or dirt, snippets of hair, or other tiny things floating about in a dirty ship can lodge in the piercing, causing irritation, divert the immune system, and create an opportunity for infection by nastier creatures.

Our most important job as piercers is to avoid transmitting any harmful organism or bit of inorganic debris from one person to another. This is best accomplished by consciously developing a sixth sense of sterility awareness that alerts us when contamination of a clean areas or object happens or is about to happen.

Most people realize that they can't see germs and bacteria, although we all know that they can be found everywhere. Contaminates (germ/bacteria/viruses) are everywhere in the body piercing environment. They are even on our clothes. I see new and even experienced piercers, come to work with loose, baggy shirts, tops, or long hanging sleeves. When they bend over their piercing workspace or piercing tray, they drag their hanging clothes over any sterile and clean areas therefore contaminating the areas. Something so simple can still contaminate. It is a good practice to wear close fitting clothes to avoid this unintentional method of contamination.

Knowing when and how to change protective gloves in the piercing room is the first defense in preventing cross-contamination. You do not need to use an entire box of gloves on one piercing. Preplanning your piercing procedures and having your piercing tray properly set up will save your glove use during the piercing.

Generally, gloves should be used as follows. After washing your hands or using a hand sanitizer use a clean pair of gloves to set up your piercing tray. Change gloves to do the cleaning and prep of the piercing areas. Change gloves to perform the piercing. Change gloves to clean the piercing tray. Change gloves to clean with antiseptic toilettes any tools to be replaced on your piercing workstation. ANY TIME YOU UNEXPECTEDLY CONTAMINATE YOUR GLOVE(S) DURING SET UP OR PIERCING - CHANGE GLOVES IMMEDIATELY! If you get blood on your gloves, try to change them as quickly as possible. Not only are your gloves contaminated with blood-borne pathogens, blood is really hard to work in.

In the piercing room you know exactly where the clean/sterile field areas are. Anything that comes in contact with your gloves outside of that area contaminates your gloves. After you have cleaned the piercing area on your client, that area is now clean and can be touched. But if you touch your client in areas not properly cleaned by you, you have now contaminated your gloves and they should be changed.

When developing your "sixth-sense" to potential cross-contamination of your sterilized/clean area you need to be very aware what and where you touch during piercings. You must be disciplined enough to catch yourself before you contaminate your gloves.

When you pierce someone, everything becomes contaminated. The needle is contaminated, your gloves are contaminated, your workstation is a hazard, your client is a hazard, and your tools are hazards. Germs, bacteria and blood-borne pathogens are **everywhere**. You can't see them, you can't prevent them - the only thing you can do is preventing them from becoming a threat to you and your customers. It is critical that you become an expert at detecting and preventing cross-contamination.

Contamination in the Clean Room or area where you process your dirty tools raises different contamination issues. Avoiding cross-contamination in your processing area is very important. If proper procedures are not followed you will contaminate the tools, needles and jewelry your just sterilized. When this happens the contamination is transferred into the piercing room.

For example. if you autoclaved your needles, tools, and jewelry and don't prevent contamination when removing from the autoclave, storing these items, and transferring to your piercing room, you have just contaminated your piercing workstation and piercing tray. Even if you use pre-packed, sterilized piercing items, you still have potential cross-contamination issues with unpacking, storage and transfers of these items.

Let me caution you about pre-sterilized, pre-packed piercing setups, and pre-packed, sterilized, one-use only disposable tools. They can easily be contaminated because most people forget about the exterior of the package is almost always contaminated from handling, packing, storage, or unpacking. In other words you can be sure the package is contaminated. You can only be sure of the handling and storage of the packs once you get them. You have no idea how the packs were handled before you received the packs.

Since you must assume every package is contaminated, you might consider handling the situation this way. The packs I have seen have a plastic back and a removable paper enclosure. Using new gloves, consider wiping the plastic back with a Cavi-Wipe (disinfectant towelette), placing the plastic side down on your piercing tray, then remove the paper cover, carefully, not touching any of the contents inside the pack. Change your gloves immediately and start preparing your piercing tray with any other piercing items you need. If your pack cannot be partially disinfected on one side (plastic side), don't use it because you cannot avoid contamination using a paper or cardboard pack.

The scope of this book is to make you aware of cross-contamination, and that it should be prevented at all costs in the piercing room and your clean room or processing area. Since you cannot be observed directly by a knowledgeable piercer, you should make every effort to know your blood-borne pathogens education.

Remember, if you touch anything with your "clean" gloves that is not clean or sterile, your gloves are contaminated, and should be changed. Think of it this way. If you contaminate your glove(s), picture Yellow Mustard instantly appearing on the tip of each finger of your glove(s). Now, it is impossible to operate with that glove(s) without getting Mustard (i.e. Contamination) on everything you touch. Everything you touch with that glove will have Mustard (Contamination) on it. If you touch anything in your Sterile Field or piercing area, you will get Mustard (Contamination) on it, and now you have to deal with a contaminated piercing tray. Avoid at all costs, bringing contamination to your piercing workspace during your piercing procedures.

If you will use the mustard VISUALIZATION concept, it will help you quickly recognize when cross-contamination occurs, therefore, helping your to avoid cross-contamination. Cross-contaminations is viral. It can quickly spread far beyond the initial contamination point of contact.

© 2010 Jerry Frederick/Body Creations - ALL RIGHTS RESERVED

Chapter 7 - Clean to Contaminated

Throughout your body-piercing career it will be necessary to carefully deal with your piercing environment, room, and instruments as they pass through the stages of sterile to clean to contaminated condition.

Therefore it is imperative that you thoroughly understand what is sterile, very clean, clean, not clean, dirty or contaminated. During the piercing process you must know how your environment, the piercing room and the piercing instruments go through this process and how you deal with it so you don't contaminate your client, yourself, or surroundings.

Years ago when I went through the Gauntlet Body Piercing Training Seminars they devised a color chart to teach us the concept of providing a safe environment for you and your clients, and understand the meanings of the terms sterile, clean and contaminated.

We will use colors to help you visualize how this works. For instance sterile will be white and contaminated is dark red with shades in between. It works this way. When a lighter color item comes in contact with a darker color, that item (lighter color) now becomes that darker color and can pass it (results from that contact) on until it is disinfected or sterilized.

We will assign the follow colors to the following conditions.

White is Sterile
Palest Pink is Very Clean
Pale Pink is Clean
Pink is Not Clean
Red is Dirty
Dark Red is Contaminated

As a matter of practice nothing darker than pale pink should ever come in contact with a piercing directly or indirectly. You should avoid red items with bare hands. If you touch red items you should wash you hands immediately. Look at the list and see Dark Red is Contaminated, so never touch Dark Red items with bare hands.

Here is a description of the following colors and their condition with examples of the pertinent items you will come in contact with in the piercing room, clean room and jewelry display area.

White - Is Sterile which means No Living Matter. Examples are freshly autoclaved instruments, jewelry, needles, etc. in unopened, sterile bags, untouched.

Palest Pink - Is Very Clean which means only very small quantities of airborne matter. Examples are sterile instruments just removed form their bags. Disinfected instruments only touched with freshly gloved hands, trays or surfaces immediately after disinfection. Jewelry that has just been removed from disinfecting solution. Bagged "sterile" instruments after several weeks in storage.

Pale Pink - is Clean which means only small quantities of airborne matter. Examples are pre-sterilized corks, rubber bands, non-sterile latex gloves, tissues, cotton swabs, etc. stored in protective containers and only touched with freshly gloved hands. Surface of "sterile" field, only touched with freshly gloved hands if paper is changed daily. Needles, forceps, disinfected jewelry, etc. after several minutes in open air, unused. Surface of skin immediately after Techni-Care Surgical Scrub or similar product. Hands - immediately after washing with anti-microbial scrub.

Pink - is Not Clean meaning normal levels of airborne matter. Examples are needles, forceps, corks, rubber bands, etc. after extended exposure to open air or frequent handling. Clothing, surfaces, instruments, neither contaminated with blood-borne organisms, nor recently disinfected. Unused jewelry prior to sterilization/disinfection. Piercing room furniture, etc.

Red - is Dirty which means high levels of airborne matter and possible presence of blood-borne matter. Examples are floors, countertops, sinks, doorknobs, light switches, and other areas that may have been exposed to blood-borne contaminates, either directly or indirectly. Unbroken, un-cleaned skin. Frequently handled display jewelry, phones and money.

Dark Red - is Contaminated which means high levels of airborne/blood-borne matter, bodily fluids, new or old. Piercings new or healed. Broken skin of any kind. Used piercing instruments, used disposable piercing needles. Previously worn jewelry.

If you thoroughly grasp the concept of how sterile items pass through to become contaminated until re-sterilized you can avoid cross-contamination by providing you and your clients with safe piercing environment.

© 2010 Jerry Frederick/Body Creations ALL RIGHTS RESERVED

Chapter 8 - Autoclave Your Most Important Instrument

As a body piercer, a properly working autoclave is your most important instrument. Yes, even if you are using pre-sterilized, prepackaged piercing kits or any form thereof. Pre-sterilized, pre-package piercing set up trays do not include any of the tools or instruments you will be using with many piercings, and those tools must be sterilized after each use.

We will deal with the pre-packaged items later in this chapter, but since you need an autoclave, let's see how we can get you into one.

If you can afford it, buy new, no question about it. If you can't afford try used (refurbished) equipment. If you live in or close to a large city you may be able to find a good autoclave from a local medical equipment repair service. These companies are good to know in case you need repairs on your autoclave. Autoclaves work for years without major maintenance or repairs. That is why the used ones sometimes sell at a premium.

There are Medical Repair Companies that buy used equipment from doctors and hospitals. They refurbish the equipment (autoclaves) and resell them. If they don't have any for sale, they may be able to direct you to someone else locally that sells used autoclaves or repairs them.

You can also look locally in Craig's List online. If that doesn't work look on eBay under autoclaves and you will find a lot of offerings. You can also do an Internet search using the search term "used autoclave", and you will find companies who refurbish and sell used autoclaves.

If you buy used, make sure the autoclave is sold with the proper trays and rack for that specific autoclave, the timer and pressure gauge is in proper working order, the water reservoir is not leaking, and the door seal does not leak under pressure.

If you get a relatively new previously owned autoclave the door seal can be purchased and replaced from an authorized dealer for the autoclave. If you can get some kind of warranty, that would be great too . . . but realistically, not likely. Ask for an operations manual. If you don't get one, do an Internet search for "manual" using the name and model of the autoclave, download it and print off. Then follow manufacture directions for sterilizing procedures for time and heat.

There are very few actual working/moving parts in an autoclave. The only things that need to be working are the heating element and timer, and of course, the door seal must work to hold the pressure and steam inside during a sterilization cycle.

What Kind and Size Autoclave Do I Need

For body piercing, my preference of an autoclave is the Ritter M-7 Speedclave. It has the capacity necessary to handle a high volume-piercing studio. Looking on eBay they are offered in a refurbished condition between $700 and $1,000. That is a very reasonable price range.

If you need smaller capacity and smaller costs, you might look at a vertical style (upright) autoclave like the Prestige Clinical Autoclave. Used it is around $500 and does a very good job for what it is. Main problem is it does not have a drying cycle, so you have to deal with wet bags holding your tools and needles. Wet bags are porous and can be contaminated by handling and air borne pathogens until they dry.

There is also an All American 1915X stove top sterilizer ($300) that is being marketed to Body Piercing and Tattoo shops. Not sure if you can use a hot plate (so you don't need a kitchen stove) to heat up the autoclave. Obviously, this is a temporary solution to your need for an autoclave. Drying the autoclave bags after sterilization cycle is still a big issue because they can be easily contaminated until they dry. Once the bags dry, the dry bag protects the contents from air borne contaminates.

The size, kind, used or new autoclave is one of the first big decisions you will make as a body piercer. Hopefully you will make the best decision for you, however, if you buy an autoclave and find it doesn't fit your needs well enough, keep it as a back up autoclave. Having a back up autoclave can save your behind at some point in your body-piercing career.

I Use Pre-Sterilized Packs Why Do I Need An Autoclave

Body Piercing requires a lot of tools to perform all of the procedures necessary for piercing, inserting/removing jewelry, and stretching. All of these tools used in these procedures must be sterilized and the autoclave is the only way to sterilize them. It is impossible to have all of the tools, tapers, clamps, hemostats, pliers, jewelry openers/closers, and jewelry you will need every day pre-packaged and in sterile condition. You will encounter many situations requiring tools that you were not anticipating and if they are not ready for your use you are in a bad situation.

It is best if you have multiples of each tool or taper in its own sterilized package ready for use. Generally this means sterilizing and packaging them yourself, using proper storage guidelines.

Yes, Everybody Needs an Autoclave

You cannot practice sterile technique using dirty tools. Tools such a forceps, hemostats, insertion tapers, and jewelry openers/closers that come into direct contact with open tissue need to be made of surgical stainless steel or other material which will not corrode and is autoclavable. These tools should be considered one-person tools that can be autoclaved between each use.

Reusable tools are used on only one-person, then cleaned, packaged, and autoclaved. Handle sterilized tools only with freshly washed hands inside of a fresh pair of gloves.

No matter what type of pre-packaged-sterilized tools and needle set up you try to employ, there will always be items that need to be autoclaved. Jewelry, tapers, gauze, toothpicks, Medi Q-tips are just a few of the items you will use with every piercing that cannot be purchased pre-sterilized. Some type of autoclave is a must.

© 2010 Jerry Frederick/Body Creations - ALL RIGHTS RESERVED

Chapter 9 - Oops Where Is That Needle

Proper techniques in the sterilization, storage, use and disposal of the piercing needle is a primary safety concern with any responsible body piercer. The piercing room can easily be described as "controlled chaos". Meaning the piercer is performing the various steps to complete the piercing, while observing the well-being and demeanor of the piercee, and dealing with potential distractions, inappropriate comments or fainting from observers in the piercing room.

Consequently, the piercing needle is very easy to lose track of on the piercing tray before and after the piercing. To avoid misplacing the needle, the piercer should practice a routine for every piercing knowing where to place the needle before the piercing, and how to secure the needle after the piercing, This routine should be followed with every piercing.

For instance the needle should stay in its unopened sterile pouch until it is needed to perform the piercing. Once the needle is removed from its pouch, put the sharp end of the needle in lubricant for the piercing. Perform the piercing with the needle. If you follow our suggestions for how to pierce the needle will be safely corked as you complete the piercing. Immediately remove the corked needle from the piercing tray and carefully place into the sharps container without touching any part of the container.

The sharps container is a special container to store contaminated needles until disposed of in a medical waste container. Sharps Containers are plastic jars or jugs, usually red, made and sold in a variety of sizes specifically for collecting hypodermic needles and syringes, but body piercers use them for contaminated piercing needles, corks and biopsy punches (used for dermal anchors).

More Tips for Managing Your Needle

During your piercing set up you will be selecting a needle for your piercing. The pouch storing you sterile needle should be marked with the gauge of the needle and the date it was sterilized. Make sure you select the proper gauge for the needle and visually double-check the needle to make sure the needle matches the gauge listed on the pouch. Most of your clients will be needle phobic so help them out and lay the pouch needle side down so they cannot stare at the needle.

Since piercing needles are very sharp they must be handled with great care to avoid a needle stick. One of the many things you will be doing at the same time is being aware of the location of your needle during the piercing procedure.

It is not a good idea to mix your needle and insertion tapers together on your piercing tray. Have only one (1) needle out of its pouch at one time, even if you are doing multiple piercing on the piercee. Don't leave a piercee unattended with an uncorked needle sticking out of their piercing.

Inspect your needle carefully through the clear plastic film of the needle pouch for a visual verification of gauge and sharpness to avoid any defects. It is very embarrassing to use a mislabeled needle for a piercing that does not match the jewelry you are inserting. Always visually check your needle before every piercing.

Disposal of Your Needles

Dispose of your needle immediately after use, and if possible don't even return the needle to your tray. The best practice is to immediately put the used corked needle in your sharps container. This container should be in the designated contaminated area in your piercing room, marked clearly as a biohazard area. The sharps container should be kept away from your clients and remember the entire container should be considered contaminated and treated as such.

Sharps containers are marked when they should be disposed of, and how to close them for proper disposal once they are full. Call a medical waste company in your area to dispose of the sharps container. Never dispose of a full sharps container in the garbage or trash.

Never throw a needle in the trash. Dirty or clean, new or used, needles can threaten your health, as well as that of your clients and your trash collector.

Store sterilized packaged needles in a cool, dark, dry place to prevent accidental contact. Touch packaged needles only with fresh gloves or a clean tissue. When opening the needle package for use, tear open the package with the non-sharp end of the needle. The sharp end of the needle can be dulled or bent if used to open the package.

Use only one (1) needle per client, never reuse needles on another client. In my training 15 years ago it was OK to use the same needle multiple times on the same person in a single piercing session. In other words if you did a double nipple piercing you could use the same needle on both nipples. Frankly that is still true. What are you going to do contaminate the same person with their own contamination?

But that was when needles were $2.50 to $3.00 a pierce. Now the best ground needles are only between 15 and 25 cents therefore eliminating cost as an issue.

Since cost is not as issue, I suggest using one needle per piercing. Once you do a piercing and cork the needle, that certainly dulls the needle somewhat making the second piercing (using that same needle) less comfortable than the first piercing. Performing "comfortable" piercing is certainly the reputation you want, so use one needle per client per piercing.

Let's recap.

- Use one needle- per piercing- per person- per piercing session
- Carefully inspect each needle before opening
- Only have one needle out of its package at any one time even for multiple piercings are being performed
- Remove needles from their sterile package only when you are ready to use them
- Be extremely cautions with needles to avoid needle sticks
- Know where an exposed needle is at all times
- Dispose of the needle immediately in a sharps container

© 2010 Jerry Frederick/Body Creations - ALL RIGHTS RESERVED

Chapter 10 - Common Piercing Questions Answered

As a body piercer you will get a variety of questions from your skittish clients, and it is very helpful to calm their nerves, if have an engaging, knowledgeable answer for their questions.

The question you will be asked the most is Does It Hurt? When I am asked that question (every day) I smile at them and say, "most people feel a little pressure, that's about all . . . you will do just fine". When the piercing is finished most clients say that was not nearly as bad as they thought, and that is almost always true. So don't be afraid of the question and deal with it head on.

As I mention earlier in this book, you have about 30 seconds to establish a basic level of trust and confidence with your client. Therefore, instant credibility goes a long way making your answers to these questions believable and useful to your clients.

For some reason I get this questions a lot. **When can I change my jewelry?** This is a little trickier question.

First you must identify what they really mean. Do they really intend on taking the jewelry out of the piercing and not replacing it? Do they mean change the type of jewelry, such as buying jewelry from a shopping mall and putting inferior jewelry in their piercing? Generally, most people are thinking about changing the piercing jewelry to some type of glitzy, dangle jewelry.

You want to remind your client to let the piercing heal before changing to new jewelry from the piercing jewelry. Of course, the best thing is to encourage your client to come back to your shop to change their jewelry. I always tell them that I will change the jewelry for free if they buy it at my shop. If you can persuade them to come back to buy new jewelry from you, you accomplish two things. First, you make a jewelry sale. Secondly, you have the opportunity to properly fit your client with the appropriate jewelry for their piercing.

Do you numb it? My answer is always NO! Surface numbing takes to much time to work and over-the-counter numbing products are rarely effective on any piercing other than a Prince Albert piercing. In addition numbing hardens the tissue making the piercing harder to perform.

Only properly licensed medical professionals can legally administer injectable anesthetics. Assure your client that a properly performed piercing will be more comfortable than having an injection to save the feeling of a piercing. Frankly, you will get the same feeling either from the anesthetic injection or the piercing.

My experience is that Doctors don't have a clue where to inject anyway. I have had nurses thinking they are really smart by letting the Doctor they work for give them an injection before they come in for their piercing during lunch time, only to find the injection was in the wrong place or totally ineffective anyway.

Don't let the numbing issue cause you any problems. Simply reassure your clients that all they will experience is a little pressure and the piercing will be over in a split second. Be nice and reassuring, it will get you a long way in the body piercing business. In addition, as a piercer, you cannot inject anesthetic into your clients anyway. Therefore, the best way to deal with this matter is by using your people skills to convince your clients they are in good hands.

How Long Will It Take Before I Can Take the Jewelry Out Without the Piercing Hole Closing?

It is hard to say. I know many of my clients want to eventually take a piercing out for work, sports, or cheerleading, etc.. I strongly suggest they resist taking the jewelry out of the piercing without replacing it with a retainer in the piercing. The body does not like a hole in it without something in it. The piercing hole will begin to shrink as soon as jewelry is removed. How much it will shrink varies from person to person.

The wisest course of action is to never leave the piercing hole without some type of appropriate jewelry or retainer in it. Remember healing a body piercing is something very new to the body. The body and the jewelry must co-exist together as the body heals. In summary, my answer to this question is most people cannot take their jewelry entirely out without the hole closing. I many cases you can re-insert the jewelry with a lubricated taper, but no guarantees. When this issue comes up work with your client the best you can. Ultimately, your client will do what they have to do. As you read the next question you will have a better understanding of how to help your client by understanding the healing process.

How Long Until My Piercing is Healed?

The healing process occurs in several overlapping stages. When dealing with problem or potentially problem piercings the piercer's observations of the healing or inflammatory signs of the piercing are very important.

After the initial piercing the tissue begins dealing with the trauma of the piercing and the potential irritation of adjusting to a new piece of jewelry in it. The tissue can become tender from the piercing, and subject to irritation or infection as it deals with supporting the jewelry. It can experience crusting and discharge during this period. This is basically the inflammatory stage of the healing process.

As a side note, you can see what types of issues the tissue is dealing with after the piercing. This should impress upon you how "unhappy" the skin becomes when inappropriately sized jewelry is placed in a piercing. The tissue will communicate with you, if you will simply observe the signs of what is happening to the piercing.

If you get a little redness around the piercing, that is normal natural healing response. The tissue is telling the body that it has experienced some trauma and it needs to begin the healing process. If the tissue is bright red and shinny around the piercing, that generally means the tissue is very irritated and something needs to be done to relieve the problem. When the tissue around the piercing turns light pink, the light pink color expands far beyond the actual boundary of the piercing, is swollen, colored pus secretes from the piercing, and may become warm-to-hot to the touch, this is indicative of infection.

The next stage of healing tests your client's patience. The newness of the piercing is over, they have passed the initial soreness, and they have become accustomed to the jewelry in their body. But the piercing is still not healed. At this point most piercing clients become impatience and begin cutting corners on their aftercare.

Normal wound healing during this period is generally several weeks, however, this wound is healing with body jewelry in it and takes considerably longer. The reason it takes longer is twofold. First, the wound must heal around a piece of body jewelry, and secondly that body jewelry typically creates minor to major irritation to the wound, thus impeding fast healing. After this stage your piercing is generally considered healed and ready for the seasoning stage.

The final stage of healing is the seasoning or strengthening of the skin cells that are lining the interior of the piercing channel holding the body jewelry. The seasoning of the piercing channel is an ongoing process, but can be interrupted if excessive wear and tear occurs to the piercing.

For more valuable information about how wound care affects body piercing, go to the Wound Care Information Network, http://medicaledu.com/phases.htm. This gives you more information on the phases of healing a wound that will help you understand how a foreign object (body jewelry) inserted into the body heals from start to finish.

Obviously, it is difficult to announce a date certain when a persons piercing is healed. When a person asked how could they tell when their piercing is healed, I respond this way. When your piercing stops crusting, and non-lubricated (dry) jewelry is tight and hard to move through the piercing tunnel, absent of any discoloration or tenderness, the piercing is probably healed (at least gone through the first and second stages of healing and your chance of infection is virtually nil)

What Are Common Types of Secretions Clients Can Expect from Their Piercings?

Shortly after a piercing is completed all types of stuff will collect in the piercing to aid in blood clotting, prevention of infection, and start the initial stage of wound healing. If you want to know what the "stuff" is then go to http://medicaledu.com/phases.htm and read about it.

As the piercing is starting to heal new skin cells are replacing the lymph and dead cells. As they are being replaced with new tissue they push out the old, dead "trash" forming a normal secretion. When this secretion hits the air at the edges of the piercing, it dries and forms a "crust" around the piercing. This is when people experience their jewelry sticking. This discharge is a normal, natural healing process. The piercing can also exhibit a little, light redness around the entrance and exit holes of the piercing. That also is a normal, natural healing response. Think back when you had a cut in your skin. A light red color appears along both sides of the cut during healing. This is normal and the light red color does not indicate problems.

Instruct your client to remove the crust with a clean cotton tipped applicator (Q-Tip) after showering or cleaning, depending upon the cleaning process used. Also tell your client not to pick the curst off dry, or use dirty hands to care for their new piercing.

The above-described discharge is not to be confused with pus. A piercing can discharge pus in response to some type of inflammation or infection. Pus is yellowish-white, thick and smells foul. Everybody has seen pus at one time or the other. A little pus can be secreted from a piercing early in the healing stage. This is primarily due to inflammation. It is generally not a big deal for a "little" pus to be secreted unless you observe other factors like signs of excess irritation that may be causing a bigger problem. If you observe colored pus, that is an indication of infection, and suggest to your client that they see a medical professional.

Where Can a Person go to Check Out a Potential Infection?

If you have chain drugstores in you area, you might make acquaintance with a physician assistant that runs the medical office in one the local drugstores. Explain what you do and what types of medical issues you encounter. Try to make business relationship with them. In other words, try to create a piercing friendly medical professional you can give a card to for any of your clients that may need help finding inexpensive medical help with a problem piercing. In addition, if the medical professional knows what is going on, they will not over-react like many doctors do by advising people to immediately remove their jewelry and never get pierced again. Doctors are lazy in their medical care with piercings and have very little knowledge about the issue of wound care healing, especially with body jewelry in the wound. In most cases they just try to scare people about body piercing.

What is the Other Secretion a Client Might Encounter in a Normal Piercing?

Sebum is the other secretion that collects in a piercing. Sebaceous glands secret sebum and are found in hair-covered areas where they are connected to hair follicles. They are also found in non-hair areas of eyelids, nose, penis, labia minor and nipples. The primary matter you will deal with is the confusion of your client thinking sebum is pus; therefore, something must be wrong with their piercing. Sebum is more solid than pus. It is cheese-like and has a distinctive rotten odor. Your dealing with sebum secretions will primarily be with genital and nipples piercings. It is especially important to clean nipple piercings to avoid sebum build up that can make the nipples tender or sore. Sebum is a natural secretion and in the absence of other indicators not something your client should be concerned with. Just keep piercings clean and sebum secretions should not be a problem.

When Can I Have Sex After a Genital Piercing?

As a rule genital piercings heal quicker than most other piercings. But they must still be protected from contamination during sexual activities during the healing process. Even if you are in a monogamous relationship you still must protect the piercing from the bacterial of your partner. That means using a good quality condom for intercourse or dental dam or kitchen plastic wrap for oral sex. A piercee will experience tenderness with a genital piercing. How soon after the piercing, sexual activity resumes, will depend upon the amount of discomfort is experienced from that activity. Patience is important, and a little creativity will get your client back into sexual activity sooner.

Will I Set Off Metal Detectors?

Highly Unlikely. If you have a collection of body jewelry in one place you may set off a metal detector. If the body jewelry is a very heavy gauge it is possible. Most people with a few piercings like face, nipples and genitals will not have a problem with metal detectors. Hand wands may be a different situation, but if you get the wand treatment, you can tell the operator where the jewelry is before they get there.

Why Don't You Use a Piercing Gun?

First, a piercing gun inserts very poor quality of jewelry that can cause numerous problems. That should be enough not to use them. Piercing guns force a blunt end of solid jewelry through the ear lobe, thereby, splitting the ear lobe open to accept the solid piece of jewelry. Tearing the tissue with a piercing gun complicates the healing process. Piercing guns are designed for ear lobes, and are certainly not appropriate for piercing other parts of the body, especially the nostril.

Will Nipple Piercings Interfere with Breast Feeding?

Our clients have not reported any problems breast-feeding with well-healed nipple piercings. Generally, the industry suggests, if a nipple piercing is less than 1 year old, the nipple piercings be removed. This is an area where you can pass on what your clients have reported to you, but the best policy is to let the woman and her medical professional make the decisions.

How Should a Piercer Handle Questions about MRI's with Clients?

Magnetic resonance imaging (MRI) is a noninvasive medical test that helps physician diagnose and treat medical conditions.

MR imaging uses a powerful magnetic field, radio frequency pulses and a computer to produce detailed pictures of organs, soft tissues, bone and virtually all other internet body structures.

Detailed MR images allow physicians to better evaluate various parts of the body and certain diseases that may not be assessed adequately with other imaging methods such as x-ray, ultrasound or computer tomography (also called CT or CAT scanning. MR information provided by http://www.radiologyinfo.org.

The concern about metal body jewelry is that it can interfere with the image quality if close to the area being scanned. Therefore, you will almost always be required to remove the metal jewelry. In many cases you can temporarily insert plastic or glass retainers in the piercing eliminating the MR imaging quality problem.

As a piercer don't fight it, work with your client to satisfy their needs. At our shop we do not charge our clients for removing or re-inserting jewelry for MRI's. Many times you will sell a retainer, or in some cases multiple retainers. Helping people with MRI issues is good for future business.

© 2010 Jerry Frederick/Body Creations - ALL RIGHTS RESERVED

Chapter 11 - Body Piercing Aftercare Suggestions

As a body piercer, you will deal every day with aftercare issues. Therefore, you need to have a good working knowledge of what simply doesn't work, what is harmful to the piercing and what will work to help heal your client's piercing.

You need to adjust your thinking about healing. Body piercing creates a clean wound in the body as opposed to scrapes, cuts or burns that most people are familiar with. Two factors need to be considered with piercing aftercare.

1. A piercing is a clean wound with limited exposure, as opposed to a ragged, ripped or torn trauma wound with large exposure to airborne contaminants. Secondly, a piercing wound must heal with jewelry in it creating the potential for irritation during the healing of the wound (piercing).

Your clients are very familiar with experiencing cuts or scrapes to their skin. In the past they used chemicals like alcohol or peroxide to kill the germs. And that's OK for a couple of times, however nobody continues to pour alcohol on their cut or scrape after a couple of days. Within a few hours the "booboo" starts to scab and that's the end of the alcohol treatment, so they never experience what happens when alcohol or peroxide is used on a continual basis to heal a wound.

Alcohol actually retards healing by breaking down the proteins in the skin, thus killing the skin cells over prolonged use. Alcohol also kills white blood cells and you need both red and white blood cells to heal. It can also dry out the skin, is flammable and has limited residual effectiveness due to rapid evaporation.

Hopefully, you can see, and help your clients understand, alcohol is great for first aid, but not for healing piercings. Hydrogen peroxide has the same negative characteristics as alcohol for healing. Consequently, discourage your clients from using hydrogen peroxide. Hydrogen peroxide will sabotage the healing of a piercing the same way alcohol will.

What Is This Red Bump on My Cartilage or Nose Piercing? Is It Infected?

Quick answer, it's probably not infected, just irritated.

2. Piercings are susceptible to red bumps around them, the cartilage, nostril, and navel piercings. The red bump looks similar on all three piercings and generally is caused the same way. Irritation is generally the culprit.

If the discharge from the bump is clear, white or slightly yellow fluid, or if the piercing appears to be otherwise normal, it is probably irritation that is causing the bump. If there is a greenish or smelly discharge with light pinkish tissue around the bump it may be infection.

What Causes That Bump?

The cartilage, nostril and navel piercings are susceptible to irritation from sleeping on them. The cartilage can be irritated from banging the telephone on the pierced ear, as well as tangled and yanked in hair, motorcycle and sports helmets and other types of pressure that create irritation.

Although sleeping on the nostril and navel piercings is the primary cause of irritation, the nostril piercing gets irritated from catching a prong from the jewelry on clothing and being yanked, or excessively removing and re-inserting the jewelry for school or work.

When these piercings get irritated the tissue starts talking and letting you know it is "pissed" by creating a bump around the piercing that can be reddish, purplish or just skin colored. This is hypertrophic scaring (not keloid) that forms to protect the skin from tearing.

If you continue to do whatever is causing the bump, it will continue to get worse. However, if it is caught quickly enough, stopping what is causing the bump, will generally clear up the problem.

The above information assumes that the piercing was not done with a piercing gun, wearing thin, inappropriate jewelry in the piercing, or wearing jewelry too tight in the piercing. Those things are almost sure to cause a bump on the piercing.

After eliminating the cause of the irritation, you can try some or all of the following ideas to help the bump to go away.

Make a sea salt hot compress by dissolving 1/8 teaspoon of sea salt in 8 oz. (a coffee cup) of very hot water. Dip a clean washcloth into the hot water. Place the folded cloth over the entire piercing area using light pressure for 15-20 minutes, once or twice a day. Re-dip the cloth as necessary to keep it hot.

If you observe discharge from the piercing, that is good. Using the cloth, squeeze to put pressure on the bump to remove as much discharge from the bump as possible, this relieves swelling and makes the bump feel better, helping the bump dry up.

If that does not work well for your client you can suggest using vitamin E oil, tea tree oil, or jojoba oil. You might try each product one at a time applied 2 - 3 times a day for several weeks.

If you don't have success with one product after a couple of weeks, try one of the other products for the same amount of time. Obviously, check for any signs of irritation or allergic reaction caused by a product. If that occurs discontinue using that product.

Aftercare Suggestions for My Clients?

We have found H2Ocean satisfies our aftercare needs. It is a non-aerosol dry mist sprayer that is ozone friendly. It is safe for all piercings and all skin types. It kills over 650 types of bacteria and our experience has been that it really speeds healing. The huge advantage with H2Ocean is the product delivery system (spray can). One spray on the piercing three times a day and that's it.

The convenience of spraying the piercing eliminates the excuse of can't do the aftercare, or don't have time.

You can find the contact information for H2Ocean in the Resources Chapter of this book. They have a lot of written information about the product and provide a full-color aftercare brochure for your client with each can of product you purchase.

Satin Antimicrobial Soap and sea salt soaks have been used for many years and are still effective. Find contact information for Satin in the resource chapter.

The only other over the counter product your clients may mention as aftercare for their piercings is Bactine. Among other things, Bactine has a very short shelf life because it becomes ineffective within one to two weeks after being opened. Also the analgesic contained in Bactine can cause allergic reactions in some people.

Re-Cap!

Discourage your clients from using alcohol, hydrogen peroxide or Bactine as aftercare for their piercings. Look at the market and select an effective aftercare product (one or two) that you can suggest for your piercing clients to use.

Warn your clients in advance about the risk of developing a bump on their cartilage, nostril, or navel piercings from excess irritation to the piercing. Be prepared to discuss methods to eliminate the bump should it occur.

Providing your clients with after-care assistance after the piercing is very important to gaining referrals and repeat clients coming back to your studio. Many people will try to get advice over the phone and that can be very frustrating trying to help them without seeing the problem piercing. If you can assist them over the telephone great, however, many times it will be helpful if they will come in to your studio so you can see exactly what is happening with their piercing.

If you can get your client to come into your studio, you will often sell them more products, either aftercare products or maybe new jewelry. In addition you can actually see if there really is a problem with the piercing. Many times the client freaks about their piercing for absolutely no reason. Of coarse, you always have to consider that family and friends sometimes try to scare them out of the piercing by telling them they have a problem with the piercing.

Seeing your client face-to-face is always your best option.

© 2010 Jerry Frederick/Body Creations - ALL RIGHTS RESERVED

Chapter 12 - What You Need to Know About Licensing & Certification

Many of you are concerned about licensing. You want to know what is it and how to get it for body piercing in your area.. The information on licensing is exploding and changing every day. At this point most states and municipalities are creating some type of licensing requirements for body piercing shops.

There are no universal standards for licensing body-piercing establishments across the country. Consequently, who knows what agency or person in your area controls body piercing businesses? One city in Minnesota, you go to the City Clerk, In another city you go to the Department of Health. One state has a Health Licensing Agency you apply to. As you can see there are a variety of places you may need to research to find what you need in your local area.

It might help for you to understand what licensing and certification really are, so you will know exactly what you are searching for.

LICENSING:

A license is a permission to do something that otherwise is forbidden. In most cases, a license is required or mandatory for engaging in that activity. For instance, a driver's license is considered mandatory to drive a car on the public roads.

A license is given by the government, and is a governmental privilege. It therefore presumes that the activity in question is a privilege, not a right. The privilege may be bestowed by the federal, state or local government. A license involves the police power of the state. That is, if one violates the licensing law, either by acting without a license, or failing to uphold the rules governing the license privilege, on is subject to prosecution under the civil or criminal laws of the governing body.

CERTIFICATION:

Certification is a statement or declaration that one has completed a course of study, passed an examination, or otherwise met specified criteria for certification. Certification is NOT a permission to act, but rather a statement of completion or qualification.

Certification is a private matter, issued by a private organization, and generally costs a lot of money and time for training to get the certification. It does not involve the police power of the state, and is not a state privilege.

Certification is based on the premise that there is a right to work. Certification only provides the consumer with more information about a practitioner. It also gives practitioners a way to increase their competency through a course of study and exams, and to advertise or inform others of their completion of this course of study.

What Can I Expect About Licensing and Certification As A Body Piercer

If a state has any regulations about body piercing they will be similar to the State of Oregon. Oregon licenses body piercing technicians and body piercing facilities.

Basically Oregon's regulations for body piercers are as follows:

Body piercing technicians perform piercing services, including earlobe piercing, in licensed facilities. Body piercing technicians must be registered and adhere to stringent universal precautions for sterilization of needles and equipment, biohazard waste disposal and infection control practices formulated to state and national standards.

They also require current training in basic first aid, blood-borne pathogens and aftercare procedures. This is far more than most states require. In reality I have been informed that training in aftercare procedures is simply your manager stating they have trained (informed) you of their aftercare policies.

The purpose of certification is mainly to set standards, educate practitioners and inform the public.

For instance, acupuncturists have a national certifying agency, BUT certification with that agency is NOT a requirement to practice acupuncture in any particular State.

In body piercing there is not even a national certifying agency, any regulations on body piercing rest with the state and local authorities. Even in the Oregon example on body piercing regulations, those regulations are no stronger than the requirements for joining and operating as a member of the Association of

Professional Piercers (APP). The APP requires you to participate in classes found locally for basic first aid and blood-borne pathogens training every year. They offer excellent aftercare information that is free of charge to members. In addition they demand that members adhere to OSHA standards for universal precautions for sterilization of needles and equipment, biohazard waste disposal and infection control practices.

What You Really Want is for Someone to Certify That Your Know How to Pierce

As you can see regulatory agencies only license and certify your business, your place of business, sterilization procedures, and that you are trained in basic CPR, blood-borne pathogens, and some type of aftercare.

Nobody actually licenses or certifies that you actually know how to pierce. This is like licensing a brain surgeon to practice universal precautions in the operating room, but requiring no training for actually operating on the brain. You could have confidence the surgeon would practice sterile procedures, but not required to have a clue on techniques and skills of brain surgery.

In the body piercing industry, this is exactly what is happening. Government demands you use sterile procedures (which is a good thing), but does not demand you actually know the skills of piercing (doing an invasive procedure) a person's body.

It is not required that you actually know how to select proper jewelry, place or position a piercing, mark the piercing, properly clamp or stabilize the tissue to be pierced. It is apparently not important that you even know how to hold a needle or complete a piercing by inserting jewelry. They don't even require any standards for the quality of jewelry your are inserting into your client's bodies.

There is no governing body (federal, state or local) that issues a license (privilege) or certification (a statement of completion or qualification) to anyone for engaging in the actual techniques, procedures and physical skills of piercing the body. In the body piercing video training found at http://www.how2pierce.com we offer (if requested) a Certificate of Participation in the body piercing training program. Video training is self-directed so no one is present to supervise and verify your completion of the training or your competency in body piercing.

Although it may give you some temporary confidence, you don't need a certificate in body piercing . . . you need working knowledge of body piercing. When you have knowledge people will have confidence in you and you will never need a certificate hanging on your wall. Body piercing is a personal, face-to-face business. You must establish confidence and rapport with your clients. If you do that successfully, they will be your repeat customers for as long as you are in business.

You have to do your own local research

Every locality either has some regulations, or none at all. Your local government may require only a business license, but that is NOT a license for body piercing - it is just a license to operate a business in that locality and that may be all that is required for you to start piercing (that license if more for collecting taxes than regulation). Other localities require more to operate a body piercing business. Therefore, it is your responsibility to inquire as to the laws, codes, and regulations in your particular area.

Here are some guidelines on how to research body piercing regulations in your area. If you know someone in the body piercing or tattoo business ask him or her. If they will not tell you then you might consider becoming a detective. Go to a body piercing or tattoo shop as a prospective client. Ask about a particular piercing, how they do it, how much is it, and casually ask DOES THE CITY(your city) OR STATE (your state) REGULATE THE CLEANLINESS AND STERILITY OF BODY PIERCING SHOPS HERE IN (Your Local Area)?

If there is regulation in your area, a shop would likely give you that information because they know they must operate under the guidelines or they could potentially lose the ability to operate in that locality. So giving inaccurate or false information could jeopardize their ability to operate. If there is regulation, a shop would probably be proud of the fact they do have some guidelines to operate under and that would be a selling point for them to attract you acting as a prospective piercing client. Obviously, if they say yes there is regulation, find out who regulates it in your area, and you are off and running.

If there is regulation in your area, it should not be difficult to get the information because the industry is more professional and not afraid of giving information that they comply and operate under industry standards on body piercing. If they try to hide the information, that is a good indication there are no guidelines for your area, and they want to withhold that information to keep you from setting up shop and becoming their competition.

If all of this fails, go to your local city clerk (generally in the courthouse) and ask the staff if they have any regulations on body piercing. Go to the Mayor's Office and ask them. If they don't know, ask their suggestions of who might know. Ask local or state public health officials. Correspond with the Association of Professional Piercers to see if they know anything about your local area. Look up Tattoo Associations and ask them. Tattoo groups are far more developed organizationally than body perching groups. Research and ask questions in Online Forums on body piercing and tattooing in your area.

Cosmetologist, estheticians, and permanent makeup artist are good centers of influence that may guide you in the right direction for governmental regulatory agencies in your area.

I have given you many ideas on researching body piercing regulations in your area. It may take a little time to get this information, but it is well worth the effort.

At this time regulation across the country is so inconsistent, it is incumbent upon you to personally check your city and state for applicable regulation and not depend upon any other source for this information using the information provided above to get your looking in the right direction.

© 2010 Jerry Frederick/Body Creations - ALL RIGHTS RESERVED

Chapter 13 - Jewelry Standards in Body Piercing

Jewelry used for body piercing must conform to certain quality standards to avoid irritating a person's skin. Your clients need to be informed of the reasons you are using the jewelry you. It gives them confidence that you are inserting the finest quality jewelry in their piercings. It also justifies your prices and confirms your professionalism as a piercer.

The following article is an excellent overview of the materials body jewelry is made of, and craftsmanship to necessary to create quality body jewelry. Ron Fante is from The Body Wire Company that sells steel wire to many of the top body piercing jewelry companies in the United States. I think Ron has a neutral view and not dog in this race. That means everybody in the piercing industry has an opinion on steel jewelry. Some insist you use only ASTM 316 LVM(F-138). Others feel that 316 LVM is completely sufficient, while others feel 316 L is all that is necessary. Hence the debate within the body piercing industry as to what is the minimum quality of body jewelry used.

Read this report and make your own decision. Again this is basically an unregulated business and no one can tell you what is the best material to use for your jewelry. As with many things in the body piercing industry you must make the most informed decision and live with it.

This is the article written by Ron Fante of The Body Wire Company, March 23, 2003.
It has a couple of dry paragraphs that don't mean much to us as laymen, but I encourage you to read the entire article so you will have a fundamental understanding about the jewelry you use in your piercing business.

I understand that the debate on 316L & 316LVM continues in the piercing industry. I'm not quite sure if I can clear up all the issues, but I'll tell you what I know, hopefully it will help resolve a few misconceptions.

First of all it's important to understand the relationship between ASTM, 316LVM, 316L and Cleanliness/Inclusions. The most common versions of 316l and 316LVM generally meet the requirements of ASTM-A-580, ASTM-A-276, ASTM-A-479 and QQS763. They also typically meet the Inter-granular Corrosion Resistance requirements of ASTM-A-262 Practice E if annealed correctly. However they do not meet the requirements of ASTM-F-138. This specification is unique in that ia has a modified chemistry (much different than standard

316LVM and 316L) and more stringed cleanliness requirements. But most importantly, it has inclusion limitations.

Inclusions can be defined many different ways, but typically they are internal in the form of stringers. Inclusions are not limited to internal structure. They can be apparent on the surface also. Any surface imperfections can be a detriment to the materials end use. Surface imperfections can take the form of stringers, pitting and even scratches. The vacuum melting process can alleviate stringers (type of inclusion) and impurities in the material such as sulfur, phosphorous, and unwanted gases (Note: There are other types of re-melting processes besides vacuum melting (VM used to achieve the cleanliness/inclusion requirement of F-138).

Pitting, scratches and other surface imperfections must be eliminated by surface removal and good polishing technique. Most experts recommend that martial used for implants and must comply with ASTM-F-138 even though standard 316L was used for many years before they switched to Titanium and 316LVM (F-138) material.

This is apparent due to the fact that the second largest melting mill of stainless steel in the country (Crucible Steel), lists "surgical implants" as a typical application on their standard 316L data sheet. What does that mean? I believe the answer to this question is understanding "Nonmetallic Inclusions" and how they effect the material.

These inclusions are imperfections in the material caused by nonmetallic elements that have a tendency to segregate, forming a stringer. THESE IMPERFECTIONS CAN HARBOR BACTERIA (very bad thing for body piercing jewelry).

Therefore, surface preparation during the jewelry manufacturing process becomes critical. The surface must be relatively free of inclusions. It is true that the Vacuum Melt (VM) process reduces nonmetallic inclusions, but F-138 is not necessary to accomplish this. The F-138 specification is considered implant quality primarily do to the increase in nickel content which is added to insure that the material will not become magnetic during cold working in the manufacturing process.

Standard 316L and 316LVM has a lower nickel content and is generally at the low end. It's important for an implant to be nonmagnetic for obvious reasons.

BODY JEWELRY IS NOT AN IMPLANT (it can be easily removed from the body for MRI's etc.)! Therefore, standard 316LVM is more than adequate for this application (for body piercing).

I cannot over emphasize this point. It is absolutely critical that the surface is polished adequately so it is free of imperfections caused by inclusions or otherwise. This is most probably why the APP (Association of Professional Piercers) recommends 316LVM material. I can only guess why they also recommend ASTM-138.

It may be because they don't understand the relationship between 316LVM and F-138. I have been told that there are some States that have mandated F-138 for body piercing. If this is true, I feel this is a precautionary decision made for the same reasons or because they are not certain as to the extent the material is exposed to blood and tissue.

If a jewelry manufacturer has any doubts as to their ability to prepare the surface of their product adequately, then upgrade to 316LVM or 316LVM to the F-138. I often hear comments about the Chromium oxide layer on the surface of 316LVM F-138. This is true, but I feel clarification is needed. ALL STAINLESS STEEL HAS A CHROMIUM OXIDE LAYER ON THE SURFACE.

This is one of the primary reasons stainless steel resists corrosion. The combination of Chromium, Nickel and Molybdenum allows for different degrees of corrosion resistance. In the case of 316L or 316LVM more Chromium and Nickel is added for this reason. (A minute amount of Nickel is added to the jewelry to prevent the jewelry from corroding in the body). Molybdenum is also added to help the Chromium and Nickel do their job.

In closing I would like to add that I believe some of the problems in the industry exist because of poor processing of the material. I know of many in the industry that heat the material after forming in an effort to make it softer. This will most likely ruin the properties the material was designed to develop. A certified heat treater should always be used whenever you desire a softer material. Atmosphere Time and Temperature is critical when annealing (softening) this type of material. Many things can be effected adversely if improperly annealed, such as surface imperfections (pitting), inadequate corrosion resistance and grain structure. These are important factors that will effect the end user adversely.

A few comments on the above article . . . all of the well-known body jewelry manufactures supply at least 316LVM jewelry. Any manufacturer you buy from should be able to supply you with a metal certification that they use 316LVM stainless steel to make their jewelry. You can ask them to supply you with a copy of a metal certification to keep in your records. This information can generally be found in a manufacturers jewelry catalog in the explanation of their terms and conditions.

I use annealed jewelry because it is soft and can be manipulated by hand in the body without using tools to bend it. When tools become necessary to bend jewelry that has been inserted in the body, you run the risk of slipping off the jewelry as you bend it possibly hurting your client or scratching the jewelry. Either result is unfortunate and preventable with annealed jewelry.

You will be asked about Nickel in your jewelry from people with sensitive skin. You can obtain nickel-free jewelry but it is very limited in selection and expensive. In my 15 years of piercing I have only had 3 people who claimed to have sensitive ears that could not wear 316LVM Stainless Steal in their navel or other body areas. So sensitive skin is real, but very few people claiming sensitivity to anything other than nickel-free jewelry really have trouble with quality steel body jewelry in my experience.

Stocking some nickel-free titanium of your most popular jewelry selections is a good idea and can prevent loosing a piercing when a client will not try steel.

Chapter 14 - Successful Stretching Discussed

Stretching is an area of your body piercing business that you can get the most grief over. People will generally follow your advice on healing a piercing. However, very few people religiously adhere to your suggestions for stretching parts of their body's especially the ear lobes.

People become very impatient when stretching is involved. Most times their expectations are completely unreal. They want to go from an 18 gauge to a 6 gauge in one day. One problem is there is always some "Swinging Charlie" out there telling people he did it to himself or he can do it for your clients. Dealing with unprofessionals in your area giving people unrealistic expectations is a problem you will have to cope with and overcome.

The Key to Successful Stretching is Time

Tissue needs time between stretches to adjust, heal and create new skin cells. You cannot force the tissue to do what it does not want to do without unhappy results. There is no substitute for time as you stretch. The longer between stretches, the easier and more successful each stretch will be.

The body piercing industry generally agrees that stretching one size per month is a good rule of thumb to follow. If you allow your client to talk you into being too aggressive, it can disappoint both of you. You are the professional and should give and try to persuade your client to follow your suggestions.

Let your Clients Know That Some Stretches Are Easier Than Others

For instance earlobes are easier to stretch than nipples, or cartilage. My experience with the Prince Albert piercing is they are very peculiar in that the PA can be very stubborn one day and not the next. If it's ready OK, but if the PA doesn't want to stretch I don't care how much power you exert, the taper cannot be forced through the piercing. If you fail at the stretch, try a couple of weeks later, it might be in the mood by that time.

Remember this and make your client aware of the following. Although the gauge of jewelry is measured in diameter, the tissue you are stretching feels the circumference of the jewelry. Which means that the circumference of the jewelry increases at a greater percentage than the jewelry gauge increases in diameter.

The best way to demonstrate this to your client is to put a plug the size your client has now on top of the plug your client wants to stretch to. This is a very good visual for your client to see the increase in the stretch, especially when your client wants to skip a size.

When you do not allow enough time between piercings, you impede the tissue from regenerating and future stretches may tear the tissue or retard its elasticity due to scaring. The best policy is go slow when stretching.

A heat compress will aid your stretching efforts. Put hot water on an absorbent disposable cloth to make a hot compress on the area you are about to stretch. This can be very helpful by causing the tissue to expand and become soft making it potentially more comfortable on your client. Suggesting a daily sea salt hot compress to your client can also speed healing and circulation.

Always lubricate the taper and jewelry you are using for insertion. Water-based lubricants (Bacitracin) can cause less irritation, and cleans up easily.

Suggest to Your Client the Importance of Keeping the Stretching Area Clean

Suggest your favorite aftercare product to keep the piercing clean and free of bacteria. Remember the discussion of sebum. This is a common secretion with stretched tissue and must be cleaned off when it appears. Proper hygiene can go a long way to reduce any odor of the ear associated with the stretching.

As a piercer you will be asked, "how far can I stretch and the hole close if I take the jewelry out?" You can't give them a definitive answer, but impress upon them that it may not be reversible, because the is no specific time or size of jewelry that determines what will shrink back to normal or what won't. Stretching is an alteration to the body and the area will not be the same when the jewelry is removed. In our area we have access to plastic surgeons that will repair stretched ear lobes. Our experience so far has been the lobe is reparable by the cartilage stretches have not repaired satisfactorily.

Alternative Methods of Stretching

You may find it helpful to employ alternative stretching methods for in-between gauge sizing. This can be very successful when stretching up in the larger gauges. By wrapping Teflon Tape (found at the hardware store - plumbing section) around plug-style jewelry you can increase the size of the jewelry, therefore gradually stretching the hole larger until a taper stretch can be easily used without tearing the tissue.

Another alternative method to aid stretching is wearing stretching weights in the piercing to steadily increase the size of the hole by allowing gravity to work for you. You can also use multiple rings at add weight. If done slowly adding weights can be a gentle way to stretch, or a way to speed up the adjustment of the tissue to a larger size.

As you can see there are two basic camps on the approach to stretching. One is the conservative, safe-and-slow route. The other will be the impatient type trying to get the largest possible piece of jewelry in the piercing in the shortest amount of time.

As a stretching piercer you will need to determine your approach to stretching and do a risk/reward evaluation as to best method to serve your clients while satisfying their wants and expectations.

© 2010 Jerry Frederick/Body Creations ALL RIGHTS RESERVED

Chapter 15 - SPECIFIC DETAILS & TIPS For EACH PIERCING

This is an inside look at each piercing suggesting guidelines for jewelry, as well as unique characteristics and special considerations associated with each piercing. Information provided in this work is designed to compliment the body piercing demonstration videos in http://www.how2pierce.com.

The demonstration videos found in how2pierce illustrate in detail how to mark, measure, clamp, perform the piercing, and insert of the jewelry, so I will not repeat in this book, the areas covered by the demonstration videos.

As you develop in your body-piercing career you will discover nothing is absolute. There will always be areas of dispute from someone who swears some other type of jewelry is the best for a particular piercing. Don't sweat it, there are no universally accepted piercing norms for the absolute best jewelry for a particular piercing.

From my 15 years of observations and experience, I can suggest these guidelines, and offer my opinions of things to consider with each piercing. The one place where there is absolutely no dispute or compromise is the practice of universal precautions in every body piercing function you perform.

First, let's get the marking issue out of the way. I use a fine-tipped Sharpie for all of my marking except the tongue, and other wet areas that repel ink. To mark those areas I use gentian violet and apply with a sterile toothpick.

You will find people who rail against the use of the Sharpie pen. There are many reasons I use a Sharpie pen for marking. A fine-tipped marker is unparalleled for accuracy of your marks. The marker can be reused on other piercings, and marks can be easily erased or shaped with hydrogen peroxide and cotton tipped applicator.

The Sharpie pen contains alcohol to help keep the tip of the pen adequately clean as long as it only comes in contact with unbroken disinfected skin. Before the tip of the pen touches skin, I clean the tissue with Techni-Care Surgical Scrub. Techni-Care eliminates gram negative and gram-positive bacteria at 99.99% in 30 seconds. That's cleaned enough to pierce, and it's clean enough to mark keeping the tip free of bacteria.

On the other hand, if the tip of the pen comes in contact with broken skin, mucous membrane, or any area that has not been thoroughly cleaned the pen must be discarded immediately. The pen must be discarded if touched with unwashed bare hands or contaminated gloves. Never use the pen for writing on paper if the same pen is used as your marketing pen.

I have used the Sharpie fine-tipped pen for marking over the past 15 years and tens of thousands of piercings without incident. If you strictly follow the above guidelines, the Sharpie fine-tipped pen may help you make precise marks for your piercings.

However, if you want to use a single-use disposable pen, they are available. One brand is OP-50, OP Mark Markers. You can buy them from Metal Mafia at the current price of $20.00 per box – 50 pens per box. You have two choices for marking; so don't let this become an issue. Choose one method of marking and go with it.

Body jewelry is divided into 16ths of an inch. Therefore, you must know in order of progression, all of the different lengths/diameters from 1/8 to 1 inch (Check the Resources Chapter for conversion tables). Good body jewelry wholesalers have all the lengths/diameters in stock. It is very helpful to stock all of the lengths/diameters in your piercing studio. One eight of an inch in body jewelry can make a huge difference in establishing proper fit.

For instance, I like a client to shorten their tongue barbell after the swelling goes down after the piercing. If you pierce your client with a 3/4-inch barbell, typically you can shorten the bar to 5/8-length barbell for comfortable wear. Shortening the bar helps eliminate excess irritation. Your client is less likely to bite their bar during meals if you shorten the length of the bar and one quarter of an inch makes a big difference.

The length of a bar, the diameter of the ball threaded onto the bar, and the diameter of a captive bead ring are all measured in one sixteenths of an inch. So brush up on your fractions you will be using them a lot (Check the Resources Chapter for conversions tables).

Every piercing is measured to fit the jewelry selected. The demonstration videos show you how to measure. If you don't measure each and every time, your piercings will not be accurate. Learning how to measure each piercing is vital.

NAVEL

Jewelry that works best in this piercing is a 14 gauge curved barbell ranging in length from 3/8 to 1/2. Fourteen gauge captive bead rings are also appropriate for this piercing, although healing can take longer due to excessive irritation caused by the ring.

The navel is a unique piercing. Measuring can be tricky. The tendency is to pierce the navel entirely too deep creating healing problems. This piercing is measured with the person standing up. Refer to the piercing videos to see how the marking is done. It is very important to measure for the piercing first standing then lying down. The marking lying down is where you adjust your marks so the piercing is not too deep which is likely if you only measure while the person is standing up.

Navel jewelry can migrate out of the piercing. In some cases the navel piercing just does not agree with people and it migrates out seemingly for no reason. People irritate a navel piercing by sleeping on it daily, rubbing it on display counters, and lifting kids and boxes over the navel piercing on a regular basis. Many times a navel piercing is continuously irritated by a person's lifestyle and it can migrate out.

Reconstructed navels from tummy tucks can be pierced, but the client often needs to stand up for the piercing because often times the tissue is too tight when they recline for the piercing. My experience with reconstructed navels is about 50% success rate because very little tissue remains after the reconstruction subjecting the piercing to potential migration.

NOSTRIL

I use a 20-gauge 5/8 inch shaft nostril screw. If I have a rare request for a ring I use an 18 gauge 3/8 or 7/16 captive bead ring. In my practice I rarely have any request for piercing a nostril with a ring any more.

The reason I us 20 gauge nostril screws is that it fits perfectly into an 18 gauge needle (from Industrial Strength - Sharpass Needles) so the nostril screw can be pulled through the piercing for insertion. I use the shorter 5/8-inch shaft so the bend in the nostril screw is less likely to be visible in the nostril. If for some reason the bend is visible, I tell the client to come back in one week and I will take the nostril screw out and adjust it so not to be visible. Obviously, learning how to bend the nostril screw is important to avoid visibility of the any part of the jewelry below the edge of the nostril.

Alerting your client to avoid excess irritation on the nostril piercing will help them form getting that pesky little bump associated with so many nostril piercings. Generally that comes from the client rubbing their face in a pillow while sleeping, and putting a lot of stress on the new piercing.

LIP

Jewelry is either a ring or labret stud. I suggest 18 or 16 gauge rings for the side lip and either 16 or 14 gauge ring for the center lip piercing. The labret studs can be either 16 or 14 gauge (3/8, 7/16 or 5/16 in length or diameter). The center lip piercing ring can often times be 1/2 inch in diameter.

The lip swells when pierced; therefore, you must allow extra length on labret stud or diameter on ring in the range of 1/8 to 1/4 of an inch. I tell my clients they can come back after swelling diminishes to get smaller jewelry. For instance, if I pierced using a 16 gauge 3/8 labret stud, the client comes back after the swelling is down and I put in a 16 gauge 5/16 labret post in. Depending upon the cost of jewelry, they are charged a reduced rate for the new labret post.

In this case I charge them $5 for the replacement post that I change for them, letting them keep the original piercing post, in case they ever experience swelling on the lip again, which happens. In this type of exchange, the ball end or gem end is simply put on the replacement post so they do not buy another end. They just buy the post at the reduced rate.

Here is a placement tip for lip piercings. Do not place the piercing directly into the lip. The jewelry will not have any secure tissue to anchor the jewelry, and will likely reject. Pierce into the lip line or just below so the jewelry will be securely anchored.

I have generally found that lip studs heal much quicker than rings because people will not leave their tongues off a ring. They use the tongue to play with the ring, so suggesting a stud until the piercing is healed, then going with a ring, may be helpful to some of your clients.

MONROE

I like a 16 gauge labret for this piercing so the hole in the upper lip is as small as possible and the jewelry is more delicate looking. As with the lip, the upper lip will swell; so apply the same tactics on replacement jewelry mentioned above with the lip piercing. Marking and placement of the Monroe piecing is critical to a beautiful result. There is a very good video on placement of this piercing in the demonstration videos at http://www.how2pierce.com.

MADUSA

See Monroe/ upper lip comments and jewelry selection for this piercing. This is a center alignment for the placement.

TONGUE

Jewelry is a 14 or 12 gauge barbell. Have done it at clients request at 10 gauge. My personal opinion is if client wants larger jewelry in their tongue is to pierce at 12 gauge and stretch up to larger gauges after the piercing is healed.

Swelling occurs with this piercing and you must accommodate in your jewelry selection for that swelling. In my shop the client is encouraged to return after the swelling goes down for a shorter bar. This makes the piercing more comfortable and less likely that the client will bite on the barbell during meals. Again we charge a highly reduced rate for the bar and change the jewelry for the client. You remove the ball ends to the piercing barbell and put them on the shorter bar and replace in the piercing. The client keeps the piercing bar in case they would ever need it again.

EYEBROW

Use 18 or 16 gauge captive bead ring or 18/16 gauge (3/8 or 5/16 in length or diameter) barbell with the eyebrow piercing. This is a piercing that many people have a preconceived image of the piercing and where it should be placed, and that placement is generally inappropriate. Personally I don't like using 14 gauge for this piercing because of the clunky appearance.

On the other hand, people often imagine jewelry that is too small not realizing the eyebrow piercing a very susceptible to migration. They also see the placement either to centered or too wide creating a surface piercing instead of an eyebrow piercing. The demonstration videos at http://www.how2pierce.com give you a fail-safe method for placement of the eyebrow piercing.

LABRET

Jewelry is 16 or 14 gauge labret stud in a length 7/16 or 3/8 shortening to 5/16 after swelling diminishes.

Take care to avoid placing the piercing too low. It should not be any lower than the very top of the frenulum (the little white line, web-like tissue holding the lip tissue to the chin area). This can be a challenge when the lower lip curls down. If this situation occurs, cheat up with the piercing to the lip line, if your client will let you. If you get the piercing underneath the curled lip, the jewelry may not look good to the client.

EARLOBES

Appropriate jewelry for the earlobe is practically unlimited. Captive bead rings, labret studs, quality stainless steel ear studs.

Placement is the key to a good earlobe piercing. In the demonstration videos you see the three different types of earlobes and how to place the piercing for each.
See the Stretching Chapter for information on stretching the earlobe.

TRAGUS

Jewelry for the tragus can either be a ring or mini-labret. If a ring is used, i suggest you select Fixed Bead Rings. They are 18 gauge and come in diameters of 1/4, 5/16 and 3/8 so you have options for a small tragus. (These can be purchased from Industrial Strength Body Jewelry: See Resources Chapter)

Using an 18 gauge titanium mini-labret with a gem end is a very new, popular selection for the tragus. The labret post is very small, coming in lengths form 1/4 to 7/16. The gem end selection is wide making for a very happy client. The tragus is pierced differently than any other piercing, and the demonstration videos show how to complete the piercing.

Using the mini-labret helps reduce the irritation associated with this piercing using a ring. Therefore, piercing both sides is less problematic than with the ring.

SEPTUM

Jewelry is a ring, circular barbell or septum retainer from 14 to 10 gauge. If you use a septum retainer, remind your client there is nothing securing it into the piercing and they should be careful at night to avoid losing the jewelry out of the piercing. Flipping the retainer up into the nose at night might be helpful, as long as it is not binding the piercing in any way.

CONCH

A 14 gauge 3/8 barbell is the best jewelry for the conch. 14 gauge 5/8 rings can also be used but contribute to excessive irritation during healing.

CARTILAGE

The jewelry suited for this piercing is the same as the tragus. 18 or 16 gauge rings are very popular. The mini-labret is a great choice if the person wants a shinny gem in their cartilage. The mini-labret has a small round disc attached to the back of the post that prevents discomfort to the head when sleeping.

NIPPLES / FEMALE

Jewelry for the female nipple piercing is 14 or 12 gauge rings or barbells, which accommodates for moderate play.

Larger breasted women, or women with poor circulation in their breasts (i.e. women who have had breasts surgery) can have problems with rings. Encourage barbells for these women. If a woman has had breast surgery any time in the last three or four years, or if she has a family history of breast conditions, she should probably consult her health care provider before piercing.

Women who anticipate breast-feeding in the next year should wait until the child is weaned before piercing the nipples. The constant oral contact, milk passing through the ducts, pressure and irritation can make the nipple piercing difficult. Generally, the well-healed piercing should not be a problem with breast feeding unless soreness becomes as issue.

Marking this piercing is very important. Misplaced nipple piercings can be uncomfortable, unattractive and possibly dangerous, and yes they can migrate out.

NIPPLES / MALE

Suitable jewelry is a 14 or 12 gauge ring or barbell. 14 gauge is considered the standard gauge for this piercing allowing for light to moderate play. Although a male nipple may seem to be little a 16 gauge is not a good choice for long-term wear.

The major problem I see with male nipple piercings is the placement is entirely too deep. When a male nipple appears to be very small underdeveloped you will probably need to pierce a little into the areola (the brown pigmented area surrounding the nipple) approximately 1/16 to 1/8 on either side of the base of the nipple.

You should never mark and pierce closer together than 3/8 of an inch. On the other hand, marking and piercing the male nipple to far apart (deep) can cause irritation and what we in the industry call "triple nipple" (the appearance of three nipples due to scaring.

CLIT HOOD

For a horizontal clit hood piercing a closed ring is the best choice of jewelry. The tissue stretches easily, so circular barbells and barbells can actually slip through the piercing. A 14 gauge ring is the typical selection and the diameter is determined by the client's aesthetics and functional needs. Measurement is critical to a useful piercing. If the ring is not hitting the proper place to aid stimulation, it becomes only ornamental and ineffective.

Jewelry for the vertical clit hood piercing is a straight barbell 14 gauge 7/16 or 3/8 or 5/16 in length. Many piercers use curved barbells for a vertical hood piercing. It is totally ill logical to use a curved barbell in that vertical piercing. The idea of the piercing is to create stimulation on the tip of the clitoris If the ball of the jewelry never comes in contact with the clitoris because it is curved away, how can it stimulate.

Use a straight barbell for this piercing; your client will appreciate it. Threading the ball on the barbell after the piercing is difficult because the tip of the bar is up inside the hood and hard to reach. My guess is piercers use the curved barbell because it is much easier to thread the ball on the end because the bar is curved away from the clitoris and much easier to get to.

Remember jewelry is not fixed into your body to stay in only one position. In this piercing in particular the jewelry will tuck itself into a comfortable position, assuming the jewelry accommodates that position. Otherwise, the jewelry will tuck in a manner not consistent with clitoral stimulation or simply irritation.

For the client to get the most out of this piercing, you must have precise placement using the proper jewelry.

PRINCE ALBERT

A 10-gauge ring is my choice for this piercing. A curved barbell or circular barbell is not as good a selection because the beads can get stuck in the urethra at any time, while driving or during sex.

If your client has foreskin they may experience some irritation and potential rejection. When a penis is in a flaccid state and the foreskin completely covers over the head of the penis, it is probably not a suitable piercing selection.

FRENUM

Jewelry for this piercing is a barbell and I suggest using 10 gauge 5/8 in length.

The primary consideration for this piercing is avoiding a shallow piercing. I suggest always take a full 5/8 of tissue for the piercing. Tissue lost is characteristic of this piercing, so take plenty of tissue for this piercing. When a client experiences tissue loss it is necessary to shorten the length of the barbell for comfort and utility.

This piercing is like the Prince Albert as to the foreskin issue. If the client has excessive foreskin this piercing is not the best choice. Suggest a foreskin piercing as a better choice.

SURFACE TO SURFACE

14 gauge surface bars have made surface piercings more successful. However, some placements work better than others for a surface bar. The nape (back of the neck) has been working well using surface bars. The surface bar is designed to reverse the energy of the body to push the piercing out by neutralizing it. The surface piercing is still at risk for migration even with the surface bar.

Instead of using surface bars, you can also use Tygon. It is highly flexible which reduces stress on the piercing therefore, helping the surface piercing heal. You can get hollow Tygon in 14 gauge so you can screw internally threaded ball ends into each end of the Tygon to eliminate the tube from sliding out of the piercing. The other advantage to Tygon is the ability to cut the length to fit your needs since it is sold in continuous lengths of 1 foot or more.

The disadvantage of Tygon is its porosity that allows bacteria to rapidly degrade the Tygon. Therefore, Tygon needs to be changed frequently. A rule of thumb is to change the Tygon tube approximately every 28 days. Since Tygon needs to be changed so often and changing it is a big job, few people want Tygon as a permanent jewelry selection for their piercing.

Therefore, if you use Tygon during the healing period, be aware of the jewelry size you are changing to after the healing. It is very easy to make your piercing too wide using Tygon leaving you with a big dilemma when it is time to put solid jewelry in the piercing.

Another disadvantage is a needle larger than the Tygon tube needs to be used to facilitate the insertion of the flexible tube. In other words, you have to pierce with a needle large enough for the Tygon tube to slide entirely through the needle for insertion. So the piercing is performed, the Tygon Tube is pushed through the needle, the hold onto the tube and pull the needle out of the piercing. This is the piercing and insertion process. This causes excess bleeding and more tissue than necessary that needs to heal.

If you are working with dermal anchors, make sure your dermal anchors are titanium. Dermal anchors in high traffic areas have a high fail rate. Try to find areas where they will receive as little irritation as possible.

© 2010 Jerry Frederick/Body Creations ALL RIGHTS RESERVED

Chapter 16 - Body Piercing Migration and Rejection

Throughout your body-piercing career you will be dealing with migration and rejection issues. I have had three piercing migrate on me – one piercing two times – and they were all genital piercings. The process of the body rejecting the piercings was not uncomfortable. It was a slow but continual process of the tissue getting thinner and eventually there was not enough tissue to support the piercing jewelry.

As I mentioned in the Introduction of this book, I am revealing the experiences, observations, and conclusions of my 15 years in body piercing industry and the observations of performing tens of thousands of piercings. Therefore, what I am conveying to you is what I have personally seen and observed over those years.

Piercings are placed where they are for good reasons. The primary reason is that the jewelry placement in that particular spot has a long history of successful healing. That does not mean that just because the jewelry is placed the most appropriate spot that it will not reject.

Remember, that body piercing is placing a foreign object in the body and expecting it to co-exist with the body and stay in place, regardless of external and internal stresses the body must deal with.

The main issues concerning the migration and rejection of body jewelry we will deal with in this book, are the location of the piercing, correct markings, appropriate jewelry for the piercing and basic aftercare and healing of the piercing. The companion demonstration videos in http://www.how2pierce.com point you in the right direction on placement, marking and the appropriate jewelry selection for each piercing.

As a piercer, all you can do is strive for the best piercing placement and select the best available jewelry for each piercing. This does not guarantee a successful piercing however, but this, along with appropriate aftercare instructions is all you can do to achieve a successful piercing.

What you cannot control is the health, and destructive personal habits of your clients that work against the successful healing process of their piercings. Your clients can be overweight to seriously overweight, diabetic, anorexic, anemic, drug abusers, and just generally unhealthy. All of these factors can contribute to a failed piercing. The piercer cannot control these and other factors; therefore, all you can do is what you can control.

To achieve a stable piercing you must have a change of direction or curvature in the body tissue to place the body jewelry. Examples of curvatures in the tissue would be the eyebrow and navel. The curvature in the tissue helps to hold the piercing in place. These areas are more susceptible to migration than other areas of the body.

Examples of a change in direction of the tissue are the ear lobe, tongue, lip, or nipple. You can actually pierce through these areas of the body and insert jewelry that can be secured on the front and back of the piercing, that significantly reduces the chances of migration and rejection.

Surface to surface piercings are piercings placed in the body where there is no curvature in the tissue. Piercings placed in the straight surfaces of the body have a much greater chance of rejection because the body can easily push the jewelry out of the body.

In body piercing the terms rejection and migration are used synonymously, but they are really different. Let me give you an idea of what the two terms mean.

Rejection is what happens when the body identifies a threat such as body jewelry (remember the foreign object the body must co-exist with), and begins to fight with the jewelry trying to remove it by pushing it out through the body. The tissue is healed behind the migrating body jewelry, and generally causes scaring.

Migration is the physical movement of the jewelry moving through and out of the body. The body detects a threat (the piercing) and rejects the piercing causing the jewelry to migrate out of the skin. Once this process starts it is virtually impossible to stop. The best thing to do is have you piercer remove the jewelry to prevent further scaring.

Most piercers think that rejection/migration only occurs with relative new piercings. Surprisingly, I have had clients' report piercings rejecting after years of satisfactory wear. Apparently, the body has a mind of its own.

Many clients want to re-pierce after a rejection, and obviously want to know if a second piercing will be more successful than the first. Maybe . . . maybe not!

Manage your client's expectations by giving them alternatives. Try a new location for the piercing (in the case of a navel – bottom instead of top of the navel), different kind or material for the jewelry selection.

If they choose to re-pierce in the same location, prepare them for the same results of the original piercing.

Since navels are the generally regarded as the most susceptible area for rejection/migration, you need to be aware of a few things you can do to avoid this process.

The weight of the jewelry can adversely contribute to the failure of the navel piercing. Heavy dangle jewelry may not be appropriate for daily wear. The weight may cause unnecessary stress on the piercing and may get caught in clothes and furniture that can further traumatize the piercing.

Try wearing the fancy heavy jewelry for special occasions and parties. Wear simple, lightweight jewelry for all other times.

Other options for the navel are a change of material from stainless steel to titanium, niobium or PTFE jewelry.

Working with the issue of rejection/migration is a work in progress. There are no absolutes to correct the problem, so use the ideas mentioned above and practice careful observation so you can help your current and future clients.

This information should arm you with the knowledge and preparation to handle this issue with your clients. It is going to happen, so learn to deal with this matter in a professional manner.

© 2010 Jerry Frederick/Body Creations ALL RIGHTS RESERVED

Chapter 17 - Bloodborne Pathogens & Infection Control for Body Piercing

When starting out as a body piercer, everybody wants some kind of certification to show their clients' that they have achieved something. The first certification you need is to get your Bloodborne Pathogens /Universal Precautions and CPR Certifications.

It is not very expensive and relatively easy using online training sources. Another popular source for this training, and maybe cheaper, is to contact your local fire department and see if a fireman is offering the training and testing. It is very common for firemen to offer this service.

Obviously the Red Cross offers CPR training and certification. Online you can get the training at http://www.ProFirstAid.com .

If you state or city has a requirement for these certifications, then, they probably can give you the name(s) of people in your local area that offer these services.

If not, I have listed below an online course that has the things you should be looking for in an online certification course. The link to this course is listed below. It is $125 for the course that is not too bad; just inquire if the certificate is included in that price.

As with all the resources I mention in this book, I have no financial interest in your participation with any of the vendors.

This Is The Type of Course Your Need for Universal Precautions Training

This course provides training as required by OSHA's Bloodborne Pathogens Standard (29CFR 1910.1030). Material covered in the course includes definitions of bloodborne pathogens, modes of transmission, universal precautions, engineering and work practice controls, exposure control plans, hepatitis B vaccinations, and other information needed to the safety of the tattoo artist or body piercer. A special section on infection control has been added to this course.

This course can be used as introductory training as well as satisfying OSHA's annual refresher requirement.

Note that the standard requires an opportunity for you to ask interactive questions and receive answers from the person conducting the training session. OSHA was asked if having a trainer available to answer any questions via email was considered to be in compliance with this requirement. In an interpretation letter OSHA states that "it is critical that trainees have an opportunity to ask and receive answers to questions where material is unfamiliar to them. Frequently, a trainee may be unable to go further with the training or to understand related training content until a response is received." Therefore, it is OSHA's policy that using an email system to answer questions is NOT considered direct access to a qualified trainer. If the qualified trainer is available through an interactive on-line exchange or via phone communication whenever a question arises, this is considered acceptable.

This training course complies with the requirement by having an online chat (AOL screen name: eduwhere) available at 1 pm - 5 pm every Tuesday (Eastern Time), 9 am - 11 am every Wednesday, and by scheduled appointment, with a toll free number to call if you have questions (866-523-9108

http://www.eduwhere.com/coursedescription.php?courseID=28

Who Should Take This Course

Persons engaging in permament cosmetics activities who are exposed to blood and other potentially infectious materials (OPIM) while performing their routine work functions need to receive bloodborne pathogens training. This includes:
- tattoo artists
- body piercers; and
- permanent cosmetologists

Objectives

After completing this course, participants should be able to:
- identify common bloodborne pathogens, their paths of transmissions, and symptoms of the disease
- know what an exposure control plan is, what it contains and where it is located
- recognize tasks which may lead to exposure of bloodborne pathogens and measures to take for protection
- the steps to take following an exposure incident

- what is provided in a post-exposure evaluation and follow-up
- explanation of the color coding and symbols used for biohazards
- know the basics of infection control

Topics

Topics include:
- Introduction to bloodborne pathogens
- Bloodborne diseases
- Exposure control plans
- Personal protective equipment and housekeeping
- Hepatitis B vaccinations
- Post-exposure evaluation and follow-up
- Information and training requirements
- Recordkeeping
- General safety practices - including infection control

Instructor – Lori L. White

Ms. White is one of the principals of Eduwhere and has over 22 years of experience in the environmental industry. This includes 10 years working for an environmental laboratory that performed analyses environmental matrices such as soil, water and air as well as tissue and blood samples. In addition to her hand's on experience, Ms. White has taken numerous training courses on bloodborne pathogens and related topics to stay current with developments in the field, and she is an OSHA approved instructor. Ms. White received a BS in Chemistry from Saint Mary's College, Notre Dame, IN and completed a year of graduate level studies in analytical chemistry at the University of North Carolina at Chapel Hill.

Contact Hours

0.67 Industrial Hygiene CM Point (ABIH, Approval #10-073)
Approved by the Society of Permanent Cosmetic Professionals.

http://www.eduwhere.com/pdh.php (4.0 Professional Development Hours (PDH)

4 Contact Hours

This represents the estimated time to complete the online course, including exercises. Actual times may vary from user to user.

© 2010 Jerry Frederick/Body Creations ALL RIGHTS RESERVED

Chapter 18 - Dealing with Problems, Emergencies & Needle Sticks in Your Piercing Room

You are the ultimate leader in your piercing room. The more confident and assured you are the fewer problems and emergencies you will experience. No matter how confident you are problems and emergencies can sometimes occur with your clients and you need to be prepared for anything.

Before we approach the big things, let me cover a few tips that will help both males and females in the piercing room so you will not be obstructed from doing your job.

Fingernails should be short so you can hold and push captive beads into rings and thread on threaded beads to barbells. Long fingernails are a huge hindrance in accomplishing these tasks. Cut your fingernails to a length you think will work and try doing these tasks again to see how it works. If they are still too long, cut them shorter and try again. If you want to be a piercer, you will be working with very short fingernails to accomplish the many tasks of holding and working with very small items.

Your hair needs to be a length that will not interfere with your vision when you are bending over your clients for insertions and piercing. The length of your hair should be short enough to avoid contaminating your sterile areas. You can also put you hair up so it will not interfere with your piercing tasks.

Loose fitting cloths can contact and contaminate your sterile areas when bending over to work on your clients. It is a good idea to wear tight fitting cloths when performing your piercing duties to avoid cross-contamination.

In earlier chapters we discussed bedside manner and the verbal skills necessary to make your client comfortable in the piercing room. Now we need to deal with more advanced bedside manner such as emergencies and unexpected problems that can occur during a piercing.

Pre-screening your clients is vital. It is advisable not to pierce drunk, drugged, disruptive or unprepared clients. If you eliminate these types of clients you will mostly remove the occurrence of bad behavior in your piercing room that causes problems and creates emergencies.

However, things do happen such as excessive bleeding and fainting of your clients during the piercing process, along with unexpected needle sticks to your person. It is highly advisable to complete a Red Cross First Aid and CPR course so you will be prepared for any sudden emergencies.

BLEEDING

When performed properly, most piercings produce, at most, just a drop of blood. However, some piercings are prone to immediate and profuse bleeding. These piercings include the earlobe, cartilage, nostril, eyebrow, septum, Prince Albert, and inner labia. These areas of the body are generally highly vascular, and the tissue is pliable enough to allow blood to escape past the jewelry.

Check on your Client Release Form to see if they checked in the affirmative the question about blood thinners. If they checked yes ask them about the reason for the blood thinners and to provide you with some information that will help you decide if you want to continue with the piercing. Alcohol, aspirin and caffeine can also contribute the excessive bleeding when pierced.

As a new piercer, you are sometimes tempted to use a bigger gauge needle for the piercing than the gauge jewelry you are inserting. If you do this, even if the needle is only a half gauge bigger than the jewelry, you can count on extra bleeding.

BE PREPARED! If you anticipate bleeding have tissues on your setup tray or available in tissue holders on your wall strategically placed so you can turn and grab a tissue. I have three such wall holders placed around my piercing room for quick access.

I use a 1 oz. plastic medicine cup to hold a small amount of hydrogen peroxide to use erasing marks and for blood management, along with a 6 inch tapered cotton tipped applicator. I always have 3-inch cotton tipped applicator for heavy blood management. Watch the setup demonstration videos http://www.how2pierce.com to see how I set up the piercing tray and piercing workstation.

You can stop most bleeding with a couple of minutes of firm pressure with a clean tissue. I have discovered that letting the client hold the clean tissue to stoop the bleeding on a nostril piercing has been very effective. For some reason they know just the right amount of pressure to stop the bleeding quicker than I can standing there holding the tissue to stop the bleeding.

FAINTING

Pre-screening your clients will help immensely in avoiding fainting of your clients. Eliminate the drinkers and, if someone has not eaten in the past 4 hours, suggest they go eat and come back for the piercing, especially if it is a tongue piercing.

Always be on the lookout for signs of fainting. My clients have fainted before the piercing, during the piercing and after the piercing, as well as after leaving the premises.

Signs of fainting are incoherence, gazing off in the distance, eyes roll back in the head, sweating, and draining of skin color.

The number one rule is REMAIN CALM. Take charge and be prepared for anything in the piercing room. Always observe your client looking for signs of fainting at all times. If you see them sweating, or their skin is becoming drained of color; stop what you are doing and carefully observe your client to see if the symptoms continue. If so, offer assistance by reclining your client on the piercing table with their knees up. If they are standing up and faint, get them on the floor with their knees up.

Offer water to your client. If you have to leave the piercing room to get a disposable cup of water ask a friend, relative or co-worker to watch your client so they do not fall off the piercing table. Never leave your client unattended.

If a client faints with a needle in their body, cork the sharp end for protection before proceeding to care for them.

Talk to the fainter to even if they appear unconscious. Call their name and continue to establish communication with them. Ask what they are feeling; do they feel hot; are they feeling better . . . just keep talking to them.

If you have a cold pack available for this purpose, use it. Place the cold pack on the fainter's forehead, or if that is too cold, put it on the back of their neck.

Rule number two is DO NOT PROCEED UNTIL THE SITUATIONS IS CORRECTED.

DEALING WITH NEEDLE STICKS

As a piercer one of the real risks you face everyday is the possibility of an accidental needle stick with a contaminated piercing needle. In an earlier chapter of this book, "Oops Where Is That Needle'" I discuss how to secure and manage your piercing needles. But accidents do happen.

In the event you are accidently stuck by a contaminated piercing needle REMAIN CLAM.

If you are stuck, secure the needlepoint in a cork, and immediately tend to the stick. If you need someone to complete the piercing, ask a coworker to finish the piercing.

Note that the needle is now contaminated with YOUR blood, so never withdraw the needle back through the piercing, or reuse the needle. The contaminated needle should be discarded immediately after the jewelry insertion.

Sky Renfro organized Needle Stick Procedures into an OSHA compliant form with seven things to do in the case of a needle stick. Here are the seven things you should do in the event of a needle stick.

1. SECURE THE NEEDLE
2. If with a client, reassure them that everything is fine, and that you need to excuse yourself. If at all possible, call in a coworker to assist the client and complete any of the piercing procedure unfinished.
3. Remove your glove immediately and submerge the affected area in full strength bleach, milking the puncture in an outward motion. Do this for at least one full minute.
4. Continue milking the puncture while running warm water over the area. Wash the area with antibacterial soap, still milking the puncture as you cleanse. Do this for at least 2 full minutes.
5. Dry the area and bandage.
6. Report the incident to your supervisor and fill out the appropriate paperwork. Follow protocols as stated in your shop's Exposure Control Plan.

7. Review the incident and evaluate how the injury could have been avoided.

Dealing with these issues takes experience and a confident presence in the piercing room. That takes time, so get into the piercing room and start working, but most of all, know this material and be prepared for anything unexpected.

© 2010 Jerry Frederick/Body Creations ALL RIGHTS RESERVED

Printed in Great Britain
by Amazon